The Road
We Must Travel

The Road We Must Travel

A PERSONAL GUIDE FOR YOUR JOURNEY

Francis Chan

—— ◉ ——

Eugene Peterson

—— ◉ ——

Bill Hybels

—— ◉ ——

and more

WORTHY®

PUBLISHING

Published by Worthy Publishing, a division of Worthy Media, Inc., 134 Franklin Road, Suite 200, Brentwood, Tennessee 37027.

WORTHY is a registered trademark of Worthy Media, Inc.

HELPING PEOPLE EXPERIENCE THE HEART OF GOD

eBook edition available wherever digital books are sold

Library of Congress Cataloging-in-Publication Data

Chan, Francis, 1967-
  The road we must travel : a personal guide for your journey / Francis Chan, Bill Hybels, Eugene Peterson.
    pages cm
  Includes bibliographical references and index.
    ISBN 978-1-61795-291-3 (paperback)
  1. Christian life. 2. Christian life--Biblical teacing. I. Hybels, Bill. II. Peterson, Eugene H., 1932- III. Title.
  BV4501.3.C435 2014
  248.4--dc23
                                2013043824

The Road We Must Travel is adapted from articles previously published by Christianity Today International and published in association with Christianity Today International.

For English-language-only foreign and subsidiary rights, contact Rights@WorthyPublishing.com

ISBN: 978-1-61795-291-3 (trade paper)

Cover Illustration: Getty Images; Pingebat
Cover Design and Typesetting: Susan Browne Design

CONTENTS

INTRODUCTION

"You chart the path ahead of me and tell
me where to stop and rest."

—*Psalm 139:3* TLB

It's all about the blue highlight.

The paper roadmaps earlier generations used to fold, crease, scribble on, repair with Scotch tape, and spread out on kitchen tables, shady picnic benches, and the front seats of station wagons and mini-vans have mostly faded from view.

It's all digital now.

The new maps are bright, intuitive, up-to-date, high-definition depictions glowing on the screens of smart phones, tablets, laptops, and sleek GPS units. These are maps that don't tear along the folds, wedge themselves between car seats, or soak up spilled coffee. You don't have to turn the glove compartment inside out to find them, and it doesn't take an engineering degree to refold them. You simply type in where you are, where you want to go and . . . *voilà*. There it is. The sweet certainty of what you wanted to know.

The blue highlight.

That calming, comforting, unmistakable sapphire line overlaying your course, illuminating your way, boldly directing you from Point A to Point B by the most efficient route.

Now . . . if only we had a blue highlight in life.

Wouldn't that be something? Key in where you are right now,

enter "Heaven" as your final destination, and push the button. And there before your appreciative eyes is the course for the rest of your life—from now until you step across the threshold of glory.

But it doesn't work that way, does it? It's good and it's comforting to have a Point A and a Point B in our lives, *but where is the line marking our route?* What's around the bend? Where are the intersections? What's the mileage? Will it be an eight-lane freeway or a winding, backcountry road with a few bridges washed out along the way? How long will it take? Where are the exits, vistas, scenic byways, and rest stops?

We can ask all the specifics we like, but it really won't help. No one knows the precise route each of us will take to the other side. There may be a clear destination—and thank God for that—but there is no blue highlight marking the course from here to there.

Sometimes that's okay, and sometimes it is not. We might even identify with Thomas who, in the grip of sorrow and fear, blurted out, "Lord, we don't know where you are going, *so how can we know the way?*"[1]

Jesus, of course, told his anxious friend, "I am the way."

And he is! But he doesn't show any of us a highlighted route. That remains a day by day, hour by hour, moment by moment proposition. As Solomon noted: "The mind of man plans his way, but the LORD directs his steps."[2]

We can, however, do this much: *We can make sure we are prepared for the journey, no matter what the route might be.* This book is all about that. It's not a road atlas, it's more like a travelogue, with strong ideas and helps for navigating life. No, it's not exactly like *Rick Steves Does Europe,* but here are twelve wise, seasoned, and companionable travelers who offer thoughtful, biblical counsel for our problems, solutions to common roadblocks, and welcome encouragement for the highway that lies ahead.

Yes, like it or not, we're all on the same road trip.

But not all of us travel with peace and perspective.

With a little help from these friends, maybe we can.

PART I

ROADWORTHY

If your high-tech, carbon-fork road bike is stuck on the middle sprocket, giving you eight speeds instead of the expected twenty-four, it's no time to launch out on a fifty-mile loop through rolling hills.

If you start out on a coast to coast road trip in your seen-better-days 1990s vintage Oldsmobile only to see a "check engine" light as you back out of your driveway, you'd best give your plans some second thoughts.

God once tossed a similar challenge at the prophet Jeremiah, saying, "If racing against mere men makes you tired, how will you race against horses? If you stumble and fall on open ground, what will you do in the thickets near the Jordan?"[3]

In other words, you'd better make sure you're ready for the journey ahead of you, because you can count on some rough stretches around the corner. Whatever your mode of travel, you'd do well to make sure you're road-worthy and ready for a long ride.

In this section Gordon MacDonald, Bill Hybels, Mark Buchanan, and Nathan Conrad help us think through a few vital core issues that will get us ready for the next phase of our trek.

1

THE NEED FOR HONEST SELF-ASSESSMENT

———— ◉ ————

Each Week, Debrief with Yourself and God

GORDON MACDONALD

In 1801, William Wilberforce, member of the English Parliament and leader of the anti-slavery forces in the British Empire, passed through a severe spiritual crisis. The core issue? Political ambition. Had he mishandled the experience, it is possible that the history of nineteenth-century England would have been quite different.

Wilberforce's struggle began when a general election produced a new prime minister, Henry Addington. The banter in the streets was that Wilberforce was on Addington's A-list of possible cabinet members. Biographer Garth Lean writes that Wilberforce was sucked into the speculation and, for a while, could think of nothing else. Later, recounting those days, Wilberforce described himself as "intoxicated (with) risings of ambition."[4]

Many of us who have experienced the privileges of leadership understand such "risings" well, and ambition is just one of them. You can put abuse of power on a "risings list" along with anger, competitiveness, integrity issues, and moral temptation. And that's just the beginning. When we get enamored by a fantasy or an egregious attitude about someone or something, that mindset is hard to change. It almost never changes by itself.

For Wilberforce, the great seduction was ambition. Many of us know what it is like to be mesmerized by the lure of something bigger, more influential. Usually it's followed by the temptation to manipulate people and processes to grasp for whatever it is that the ego desires. It was a Sunday when Wilberforce finally confronted his ambition. At the end of a day of worship and solitude, Wilberforce wrote, "Blessed be to God for the day of rest and religious occupation wherein earthly things assume their true size. Ambition is stunted." The crisis was addressed.

In this brief comment, William Wilberforce references one of the great secrets of his personal life: his commitment to weekly withdrawals from the wild scramble of public life so that he could engage in worship, connection with a small circle of close friends, and quiet reflection.

It's the third of these activities—reflection—that fascinates me most about Wilberforce. Reflection is an inner conversation—discourse one generates with oneself and with God. During inner conversation, your engagement with other people is suspended. There's a time to love, to serve, to care for other people. But a time of inner conversation is personal and private.

ENGAGING IN INNER CONVERSATION

Withdrawal for inner conversation parallels the priority flight attendants express when passengers on a plane are told that if the oxygen masks appear, they should put theirs on first before helping others. That is counterintuitive, especially for mothers, but thoroughly logical.

Writer Anthony Bloom described his father as a man who knew inner conversation well. When he felt the need to do his own soul-work, he would sometimes tack a sign to his front door: "Don't go to the trouble of knocking. I am at home but I will not open the door."[5] This is not easy for those of us who are people pleasers. We are suckers for knocks on our front door.

There is a sense of inner conversation in the Psalms when the writer quizzes his deeper self: "Why are you cast down, O my soul?"[6] Or when the writer invites God's attention: "Search me, O God, and know my heart."[7]

Sometimes inner conversation originates with God. You see it in the words God uses to caution Cain: "Why are you angry? Why is your face downcast?"[8] You see it in the question God asks when Elijah flees to the wilderness in fear of Jezebel: "What are you doing here, Elijah?"[9] Then saying, "Slow down, sleep, eat, drink. And then tell me again how you got here." What follows is a fascinating inner conversation in which Elijah's inaccurate perspective on things is repaired. Paul is probably referring to inner conversation when he speaks of his "thorn in the flesh" and his frustration with it. "Three times I pleaded with the Lord to take it away."[10] But God didn't.

During his many years a public servant, Wilberforce rarely deviated from his Sabbath commitment to this inner conversation. And on the particular Sunday when he dealt with his ambition, he demonstrated why this discipline of the calendar is so important. Had he used the day for other purposes, there is no telling how his life might have gone wrong.

Wilberforce not only set aside Sundays for inner conversation, but he usually began his working days in a similar but briefer way. Sometimes I call what he did on these mornings pushing the spiritual reset button or sweeping out the heart. Once Wilberforce said of these occasions, "In the calmness of the morning before the mind is heated and weary by the turmoil of the day, you have a season of unusual importance for communing with God and with yourself."

Garth Lean comments that in the "day-to-day battle it was, more and more, these early morning hours . . . and his quiet Sundays that gave (Wilberforce) strength and perspective on himself and the world."

Wilberforce's habit of the heart has marked me greatly over the years. It has influenced my own commitment to early morning "Sabbaths" and the inner conversations I might otherwise ignore.

WHY WE NEGLECT THIS CONVERSATION

In my younger years as a pastor, I was often loaded with too much energy and too many ideas to actually believe that setting aside time for quiet inner conversation was useful. The newspaper, breakfast appointments, getting work done, seemed far more attractive. It was only as the evidence began to mount—fatigue, frustration, bad decisions, faulty wisdom—that I got the message. My priorities were out of alignment.

In my later years of Christian service, I've had the privilege of speaking to and teaching pastors from almost every denomination. I am usually not asked to talk about management or church growth or preaching. Rather, I'm most often asked to speak to the personal side of a Christian's life, where the interior battles (like Wilberforce's) occur. Central to my presentation: the place of inner conversation and the question, "What's yours like?"

DID GOD REALLY MEAN FOR CHRISTIANS TO FEEL THIS WAY?

At such conferences, in quiet encounters with men and women in leadership positions, I hear several recurrent themes, many of them alarming: "I am exhausted . . . I've run out of ideas . . . I don't know how much longer I can keep on doing this . . . It seems like everyone has a piece of me and there's nothing left for myself . . . I find myself running from people . . . My family is miserable . . . Porn (or sexual fantasy) is a problem . . . I am terribly disappointed in me . . . God seems a million miles away . . . It's not much fun anymore." The same complaints also come from some Christians who are most active in the church.

One day when I was at a New England conference center speaking on the ways in which we order our private world, I found an old book describing the history of New England Baptists. In it was a letter written in 1932 by a frustrated pastor to the executive ministry of his area: "I have been in my present pastorate seven years. I need a change. My people want me to go, although they have not yet called on me and said so. Pretty soon they may get that blunt. Attendance is down; offerings are small. I'll candidate anywhere. Just get me the opportunity."

This man thinks the answer to his problems is a fresh start, perhaps a nicer home for his family, a board of elders or deacons who'll be nicer to him.

When I read a letter like this or have the kind of conversations I just described, I find myself asking, "Did God really mean for spiritual people to feel this way? I know that suffering is often a part of the call to ministry, but is this the way things are supposed to end up for so many? Or are these descriptions a result of neglecting the inner conversation?

Henri Nouwen admitted a similar disturbance when he wrote, "What prevents (leaders) from becoming dull, sullen, lukewarm bureaucrats, people who have many projects, plans, and appointments, but who have lost their heart somewhere in the midst of their activities?"[11]

Admittedly, I may be the old guy—not unlike Nouwen in this sense—who worries too much. Perhaps I wrongly assume that most everyone is going to fall into some of the traps I occasionally fell into. But my worry increases when I see too many who have failed to take into account the indispensable need for a quiet dimension to the calendar in which inner conversation—with God, and, yes, with themselves—can happen. Lacking this, they lack resilience, sustainability, the capacity to continuously grow (or deepen) and provide spiritual leadership during the years that God gives us.

"The battle is won in the secret places of the will before God, never first in the external world," wrote Oswald Chambers. "Nothing has power over the [person] who has fought out the battle before God and won there."[12]

This, of course, is what William Wilberforce was experiencing on those Sundays: an inner conversation in the secret places.

Among my most frequently asked questions to men and women in leadership who are struggling with spiritual malaise is, "What does an ideal week look like for you? Describe for me the priority activities that fill your week." Usually, I hear a list of leader-like activities with which we are all familiar: staff meetings, sermon study, consultations with church leaders, training seminars, budget meetings, counseling appointments, long-range-planning functions. Sometimes there is comment about physical exercise (that's good) and family functions (that's even "gooder"). But what is missing all too often? Any allusion to a personal Sabbath: those times for activities that enlarge and cleanse the soul, times for inner conversation.

"What do you do in Sabbath time?" I am sometimes asked. I disappoint, I suspect, when I evade the formulaic answer. I discarded the gimmicks a long time ago. They didn't work for me. What became more important was outcomes. What do I do? Simple: whatever it takes for a renewed sense of conversion to Christ, a deeper awareness of the biblical way, an assurance that God's grace and power remain with me.

When I ask many Christians if there is time in their calendars for the pursuit of such outcomes, I get these kinds of responses:

- I'm just too busy.
- I don't have the slightest idea what I'd do if I took the time.
- My mind is too full of thoughts; I can't concentrate.
- I'm an extrovert. Being alone, being quiet, reflecting is not my thing.
- I don't get any immediate result out of doing it.
- It's boring.

Sometimes I've imagined Moses sitting in on a conversation when things like these were said. He erected a tent called the Tent of Meeting at the edge of the camp where the Israelites stayed while Moses conferred with God on the mountain. When Moses went to that tent, we are told that "the Lord would speak to [him] face to face, as one speaks to a friend."[13] That sounds like inner conversation language to me.

Although the God of the Bible is great and mysterious and cannot be described in human terms, here is an exceptional description of conversation between Moses and the God of Israel. It dares to describe God in intimate human language. But the purpose of the writer is not to make God seem like one of us; it is to express the way of inner conversation in which Moses is able to recalibrate his life.

I find it interesting that the story of Moses' tent is preceded by his devastating experience of finding his people dancing around a golden calf, a reversion to Egyptian paganism. Surprised by their behavior, he lost it. I suspect that he wanted to quit, to walk away. But based on the way the writer lined up these stories, I think we are being told that in that tent, Moses was able to say what he thought, ask about things he needed to know, and hear God renew his mission and his courage.

Moses had his tent (a certain space) and Wilberforce had his Sabbaths (a certain time). And both men renewed their strength as a result. They exemplify Paul's thought to the Corinthians when he wrote—and I use Eugene Peterson's genius for paraphrase here—"Test yourselves to make sure you are solid in the faith. Don't drift along taking everything for granted. Give yourselves regular checkups."[14]

I have found the best way to enhance such a checkup, the inner conversation, is through questions. Questions are the extension of one's curiosity, and they work beautifully as one examines his or her own soul in the presence of the Lord.

QUESTIONS FOR INNER CONVERSATION

The questions I like most search one's heart just as the psalmist mentions when he writes, "Search me!" They are meant to test the inner space of one's life and prompt conversation that leads to light.

Inner conversation begins for me by looking back over the time since my last Sabbath experience and reviewing the events that have occurred. Is there meaning in any of those events? Are there lessons to be learned, wisdom to be extracted?

My own theory is that very event, every human transaction in life, offers an insight. But it's often buried like gold or oil. It has to be discovered. Perhaps that's why busy people are impressive but often shallow. No time to mine the gold and drill the oil.

Here are far more "inner conversation starters" than you need, but these are some of the questions that, for me, begin to excavate the hidden gold:

· What have been the beautiful moments in which God may

have been revealing himself to me? And what have been the evil moments when the worst in me or in the larger world showed itself?

- What happened this week that needs to be remembered, perhaps recorded in a journal so I can return to it in the future and recall the blessing (or the rebuke) of God?

- What have my prevailing feelings been (and what are they at present)? Has there been a preponderance of sadness, of fear, of anger, of emptiness? Or has it been a time when joy and enthusiasm has been the dominant mood?

- What have been the blessings, those acts of grace that have come through others or—as I perceive it—directly from God himself? Can I express praise and appreciation (sometimes even written in a thank-you note or journal)?

- Have things happened for which I need to accept responsibility, perhaps leading to repentance? Why did they happen? Were they avoidable and how can they be prevented in the future?

- What thoughts have been dominating my think time? Noble thoughts? Escapist thoughts that woo me away from more important or challenging issues? Superficial thoughts that lead to nowhere?

- Is there a possibility that I am living in denial of certain realities (for instance, painful criticism, sloppy work, habitual patterns) that are hurting me and others?

- Are there any resentments or ill feelings toward others that remain unaddressed, unforgiven?

- Visualizing myself in the company of spouse, children, friends, colleagues: am I a pleasant person to be around? Are people challenged, elevated, enthused when I enter the room? As someone has observed, "Some people bring joy wherever they go; others bring joy when they go." Which am I?

- What is God trying to say into my life today? Through Scripture? Through other readings? What has he been saying through those in my inner circle of relationships? Through critics? What insights swirl up and out of the deepest parts of my soul? Which of them needs to be repudiated, and which needs to be cultivated?

- What are the possibilities in the hours ahead? Where might there be ambushes that would challenge character, reputation, well-being?

- What things might I do and say that would make the people in my inner circle feel more loved and appreciated?

- Am I mindful of the socially awkward, the poor, the suffering, the oppressed in my local world and in the larger world? Am I in tune with appropriate current events in the world and perceiving them through the lens of biblical perspective?

- What specific steps will I take today to enhance my growth as a follower of Jesus?

I like to ask one more question as part of my personal inner conversation. What if today is the day I meet Jesus face to face . . . either because he returns or because I am unexpectedly called into his presence? For a people who say we believe in eternal life, this is a significant question and should not be avoided.

I don't know whether William Wilberforce approached his quiet Sabbath hours with these kinds of questions. Perhaps he had a different, a better, way. What I do know is that in 1801, when he arrived at a potential turning point in his life, his habit of inner conversations helped him avoid a terrible mistake. Ambition was "stunted."

Pascal, the French philosopher and inventor, wrote in his *Pensees*: "All the unhappiness of men arises from one single fact, that they cannot stay quietly in their own chamber." I'm sure I'm taking it a bit out of context, but these words fit the point I am trying to make. People who do not take the time, who do not feel the need, who do not think they are capable of inner conversation put themselves in enormous danger. Unacquainted with the inner person, they set themselves up for possible disaster.

For many years William Wilberforce enjoyed a friendship with John Newton, former slave trader and later man of God. Wilberforce was the politician, Newton the pastor. What they had in common was their faith and their belief that spiritual power was derived, first, from the activities of quiet inner conversation a man had with God (to quote Pascal) in his own private chamber.

Newton had his own ideas of what an inner conversation was like. In his biography of Newton, Jonathan Aitken describes how Newton reduced the core of his spiritual life into five principles he believed would guide him in his leadership with people and his walk with God. He determined

- to begin and end every day with God;
- to peruse Scriptures with a diligence and attention suited to the dignity of the subject;
- to spend the Sabbath entirely with the Lord;
- to choose for my companions only good people from whom I may derive some improvement; and
- to become all things to all men in order that I may save some.[15]

That will work.

2

LOOK AT YOURSELF FIRST

———— ◉ ————

Your Toughest Challenge Is Always Yourself

BILL HYBELS

Imagine a compass—north, south, east, and west. Almost every time the word *leadership* is mentioned, in what direction do leaders instinctively think?

South.

Say the word *leadership* and most leaders' minds migrate to the people who are under their care. At leadership conferences, people generally think, "I'm going to learn how to improve my ability to lead the people God has entrusted to me."

South. It's a leader's first instinct.

But many people don't realize that to lead well, you need to be able to lead in all directions—north, south, east, and west.

For example, good leaders have to lead north—those who are over you. You can't just focus on those entrusted to your care. Through relationship and influence good leaders lead the people over them. Much of what I do as senior pastor at Willow Creek Community Church, through relationship, prayer, and careful envisioning, is to try to influence those over me—the board and the elders.

Effective leaders also learn how to lead east and west, laterally, in peer group settings. If you don't learn how to lead laterally, if you don't know how to create win-win situations with colleagues, the whole culture can deteriorate.

So a leader must lead down, up, and laterally. But perhaps the most overlooked leadership challenge is the one in the middle. Who is your toughest leadership challenge?

Yourself.

Consider 1 Samuel 30. David, the future king of Israel, is a young emerging leader at the time. He is just learning to lead his troops into battle. He's green. But God is pouring his favor on David, and most of the time the battles go his way. One terrible day though, that pattern changes. After returning home from fighting yet another enemy, David and his men discover soldiers have attacked and destroyed their campsite, dragged off the women and children, and burned all their belongings.

This would define "bad day" for any leader! But it's not over. His soldiers are tired, angry, and worried sick about their families. They're miffed at God. A faction of his men spreads word that they've had it with David's leadership. They figure it's all David's fault, and they decide to stone him to death.

In this crisis David's leadership is severely tested. Suddenly, he has to decide who needs leadership the most. His soldiers? The officers? The faction?

His answer? None of the above.

In this critical moment he realizes a foundational truth: he has to lead himself before he can lead anybody else. Unless he is squared away internally he has nothing to offer his team. So "David strengthened himself in the LORD his God."[16] Only then does he lead his team to rescue their families and what's left of their belongings.

David understood the importance of self-leadership. Even though self-leadership isn't talked about much, make no mistake, it is a good part of the ball game. How effectively can any of us lead others if our spirits are sagging, our courage is wavering, and our vision or commitment is weak?

A while back I read an article that created some disequilibrium for me. The author, Dee Hock, challenged leaders to calculate how much time and energy they invest in each of these directions—people beneath them, over them, peers, and leading themselves. Since he's been thinking and writing about leadership for over twenty years and is a laureate in the Business Hall of Fame, I wanted his wisdom.

His recommendation: "We should invest 50 percent of our leadership amperage into the task of leading ourselves; and the remaining 50 percent should be divided into leading down, leading up, and leading laterally." His numbers bothered me so much I put the article away. But I let it simmer, which is my normal practice when someone messes with my mind.

While that was simmering, I read an article by Daniel Goleman, the author of the best-selling book, *Emotional Intelligence*. Since that book was released in 1997, Goleman has been spending his time analyzing why some leaders develop to their fullest potential and why most hit a plateau far from their full potential.

His conclusion? The difference is (you guessed it) self-leadership. He calls it "emotional self-control." What characterizes maximized leadership potential, according to Goleman? Tenaciously staying in leadership despite overwhelming opposition or discouragement. Staying in the leadership game and maintaining sober-mindedness during times of crisis. Keeping ego at bay. Staying focused on the mission instead of being distracted by someone else's agenda. All these indicate high levels of emotional self-control. Goleman says, "Exceptional leaders distinguish themselves because of superior self-leadership."

As I read his corroborating data, I thought, Maybe Dee Hock's percentages aren't all that absurd!

Recall the first five chapters of Mark's Gospel. Remember Jesus' pattern of intense ministry quickly followed by time set aside for reflection, prayer, fasting, and solitude? That pattern is repeated throughout his ministry. Jesus was practicing the art of self-leadership. He would go to a quiet place and recalibrate. He would remind himself who he was and how much the Father loved him. Even Jesus needed to invest regularly in keeping his calling clear, avoiding mission drift, and keeping distraction and temptation at bay.

This is self-leadership. And nobody—I mean nobody—can do this work for you. You have to do this work yourself. Self-leadership is tough work—so tough, Dee Hock says, that most leaders avoid it. Instead, we would rather try to inspire or control our people than to do the rigorous work of reflection.

Some years ago a top Christian leader disqualified himself from ministry. A published article described his demise: "[He] sank like a rock, beat up, burned out, angry and depressed, no good to himself and no good to the people he loved."

When this pastor finally wrote publicly about his experience, he said, "Eventually I couldn't even sleep at night. Another wave of broken lives would come to shore at the church, and I found I didn't have enough compassion for them any more. And inside I became angry, angry, angry. Many people still wonder whatever happened to me. They think I had a crisis of faith. The fact is, I simply collapsed on the inside."

He failed the self-leadership test. He should have regrouped, reflected, recalibrated. Maybe taken a sabbatical or received some Christian counseling. Goleman would say that this guy lost his emotional self-control. Now he's out of the game.

A little closer to home, I'll never forget when three wise people came to me on behalf of the church. They said, "Bill, there were two eras during the first twenty years of Willow Creek history when by your own admission you were not at your leadership best—once in the late seventies and again in the early nineties. The data shows Willow Creek paid dearly for your leadership fumble. It cost Willow more than you'll ever know when you were off—not hitting on all eight cylinders."

Then they said words I'll never forget: "Bill, the best gift you can give the people you lead here at Willow is a healthy, energized, fully surrendered, focused self. And no one can do that for you. You've got to do that for yourself." And while they were talking, the Holy Spirit was saying, "They're right, Bill. They're right."

Because I know what's at stake, I ask myself several self-leadership questions on a regular basis.

IS MY CALLING SURE?

On this matter, I'm from the old school. I really believe that if you bear the name of Jesus Christ, you have a calling, whether you're a pastor or a layperson. We all must surrender ourselves fully to make ourselves completely available to God. Ask, "What's my mission, God? Where do you want me to serve? What would you have me do in this grand kingdom drama?"

Remember what Paul said about his calling? "I no longer consider my life as dear unto myself. Only that I fulfill the mission or the calling given to me by God himself."[17]

What happens when you receive a call from the holy God? Your life takes on focus. Energy gets released. You're on a mission.

I have to keep my calling sure. So on a regular basis I ask God, "Is your calling on my life still to be the pastor of Willow Creek and to help churches around the world?" And when I receive reaffirmation of that, I say, "Then let's go! Let's forget all the other distractions and the temptations. Burn the bridges!"

If you are a Christian, it's your responsibility to keep your calling sure. Post it on your refrigerator. Frame it and put it on your desk. Keep it foremost in your mind.

IS MY VISION CLEAR?

How can I lead people into the future if my picture of the future is fuzzy? Every year we have a Vision Night at Willow Creek. You know who started Vision Night? I did. Guess who I mainly do it for? Me. Every year when Vision Night rolls around on the calendar it means that I have to have my vision clear.

Every leader needs a Vision Night on the calendar. On that night you say, "Here's the picture; this is what we're doing; here's why we're doing it; if things go right, here's what the picture will look like a year from now."

We prepare very diligently for Vision Night at Willow Creek. We have countless meetings to discuss the future. We spend many hours in prayer: "God, is this what you would have?" We search the Scriptures. By the time Vision Night rolls around, the vision is clear again. But it takes a lot of work to clarify the vision and to keep it clear. Nobody can do that work for you. It's the leader's job.

IS MY PASSION HOT?

Jack Welch, the celebrated leader of General Electric, says, "People in leadership have to have so much energy and passion that they energize and impassion people around them."

I couldn't agree more. When I appoint leaders, I don't look for

25-watt light bulbs. I look for 100-watt bulbs because I want them to light up everything and everyone around them.

Whose responsibility is it to keep a leader's passion fired up? The leader's. That's self-leadership.

Last year, at an elders' meeting, a couple of the elders asked me, "As busy as you are, why do you fly out on Friday nights to speak in some small out-of-the-way church to help them raise money or dedicate a new facility? Why do you do that?"

My answer: Because it keeps my passion hot.

Last year I helped a church in California dedicate their new building. One guy took me to the corner of the auditorium, peeled the carpet back, and showed me how everyone in the core of their church had inscribed the names of lost people in the concrete. Then they covered it over with carpet. In that auditorium they're praying fervently that the lost will be found.

It was a four-hour flight back to Chicago. I was buzzed the whole way. That church fired me up! I just love watching men and women throw themselves into the adventure of ministry. It inspires me. I know that my passion has to be white-hot if Willow is going to catch it. I can't become a 25-watt bulb—nor can you.

We do a lot of conferences through the Willow Creek Association. At times pastors of flourishing churches will pull me aside and say under their breath, "I have to come here once or twice a year just to keep my fires lit." They seem embarrassed about being here so often, as if it's a sign of weakness.

I tell them, "If you're a leader, it's your job to keep your passion hot. Do whatever you have to do, read whatever you have to read, go wherever you have to go. And don't apologize. That's a big part of your job."

IS MY CHARACTER SUBMITTED TO CHRIST?

Leadership requires moral authority. Followers have to see enough integrity in the leader's life that high levels of trust can be built. When surveys are taken about what it is that inspires a follower to throw his or her lot in with a particular leader over a long period of time, near the top of every list is integrity.

A leader doesn't have to be the sharpest pencil in the drawer or the one with the most charisma. But teammates will not follow a leader with character incongruities for very long. Every time you compromise character you compromise leadership.

Some time ago we had a staff member who was struggling in his leadership. I started poking around a little bit. "What's going on here?" I asked.

Then the real picture emerged. One person said, "For one thing, he sets meetings and then he doesn't even show. He rarely returns phone calls, and often we don't know where he is."

I spoke to that guy and said, "Let's get it straight. When you give your word that you're going to be at a certain place at a certain time and you don't show up, that's a character issue. That erodes trust in followers. You clean that up, or we'll have to move you out." If character issues are compromised, it hurts the whole team and eventually impacts mission achievement.

I don't want to be a leader who demoralizes the troops and hurts the cause either. So on a regular basis, I sing Rory Noland's song in my times alone with God:

> Holy Spirit, take control.
> Take my body, mind, and soul.
> Put a finger on anything
> that doesn't please you,

Anything that grieves you.

Holy Spirit, take control.

It's the leader's job to grow in character. No one can do that work except the leader.

IS MY PRIDE SUBDUED?

First Peter 5:5 says, "God opposes the proud. He gives grace to the humble."

Do you know what Peter is saying? As a leader I have a choice. Do I want opposition from God in my leadership, or do I want grace and favor?

If you're a sailor, you know how hard it is to sail upwind. You also know how wonderful and relaxing it is to sail downwind. Peter is saying, "Which way do you want it? Do you want to sail upwind or downwind? If you're humble, the favor of God carries you. If you're proud, you're sailing into the wind. God opposes the proud."

Do you want to know the best way to find out if pride is affecting your leadership?

Ask.

Ask your teammates. Ask the people in your small group. Ask your spouse. Ask your colleagues. Ask your friends, "Do you ever sense a prideful spirit in or around my leadership?" If you just couldn't ask a question like that, then you probably do have a pride issue!

It's a leader's job—with the Holy Spirit's help—to subdue pride.

ARE MY FEARS AT BAY?

Fear is an immobilizing emotion. Sometimes I ask pastors, "Why haven't you introduced more change in your church when you know the church is crying out for it?"

I ask business leaders who are hesitating to launch a new product, "Why haven't you pulled the pin?"

I ask political leaders why they haven't taken a stand on a particular issue, one I know they have strong personal convictions about.

So often the response is: "Because I am afraid." Fear immobilizes and neutralizes leaders. Believe me, I am not above this. I remember the morning in the year 2000 when it became clear to me that we needed to launch a $70 million building program. Our vision for the future was clear. The elders, the board, and the management team signed off on it. The last step in the whole equation was for me to have the guts to pull the trigger. And you know what swirled around in my mind?

The minute you go public with a $70 million campaign, there's no backing out. It's pass-fail. I realized that everything we had worked for over the past twenty-five years, all the credibility our congregation has established in our community and around the world was on the line. Fear kept building in my heart. Why expose Willow to that kind of risk? We're cruising along. We're growing and baptizing a thousand people a year. Why are we doing this?

I am not above letting fear mess with my decision-making as a leader.

At a certain point, I just had to say, "I can no longer let fear sabotage my leadership." I reminded myself of that little verse, 1 John 4:4, "Greater is he that is in me than he that is in the world." I asked myself: Has God spoken to me? Has he made his direction clear? Is the leadership core with us? Is he going to love me if I fail? Am I still going to heaven if this whole thing doesn't turn out right? I struggled but finally I found the courage to step out in faith. The campaign was enormously blessed by God. Our church could have missed a great miracle had fear won the day.

ARE INTERIOR ISSUES UNDERMINING MY LEADERSHIP?

All of us have some wounds, some losses, and some disappointments in our past.

All that stuff has helped shape or misshape us into the people we are today. I laugh at people who say, "My past has not affected me. My family of origin has not affected me."

Leaders who ignore their interior reality often make decisions that have grave consequences for the people they lead. Most of the time, they're unaware of what's driving their unwise decisions. Some pastors make grandiose decisions that enslave everybody in their churches to an agenda that's not God's. It's an agenda that comes out of their need to be bigger than, better than, grander than.

Other leaders are incurable people pleasers. Every week they want to take a poll to see where they stand in the Nielsen ratings.

Who's responsible for your interior issues getting processed and resolved? You are. I am.

I've spent lots of time in a Christian counselor's office. I still am in contact with two Christian counselors. And whenever I think, Man, there's some stuff coming out of me that has nothing to do with the Holy Spirit, and I don't understand it, I call these counselors. I say, "I don't understand why I said what I said, why I did what I did. I know it's junk. Would you help me?" Effective leaders must get a handle on their "junk"!

ARE MY EARS OPEN TO THE SPIRIT'S WHISPER?

I estimate that 75 to 80 percent of the breakthrough ideas in my leadership over the years have come from promptings of the Holy Spirit, not through hard machinations of my mind. Some of the great sermon series or vision adjustments, value clarifications or strategy changes, some of the greatest people selections have not been due to my cleverness. It has been the Holy Spirit whispering to my spirit.

Leaders cannot afford to be deaf to heaven. Training, process, and strategy are all good. Developing your mind is essential. But ultimately, we walk by faith, not by sight. There is a supernatural dimension to leadership, and it comes our way by keeping an ear open to heaven.

I ask myself regularly, can I still hear God's voice? Is the ambient noise level of my life low enough that I can still hear God's voice when he speaks? And do I still have the guts to obey him even though I don't understand him all the time?

IS MY PACE SUSTAINABLE?

I came close to a total emotional meltdown in the early 1990s. Suffice it to say I didn't understand self-leadership. I didn't understand the principle of sustainability. I fried my emotions. I abused my spiritual gifts. I damaged my body. I neglected my family and friends. And I came within a whisker of becoming a statistic.

I remember sitting in a restaurant and writing: "The pace at which I've been doing the work of God is destroying God's work in me." Then I put my head down on my spiral notebook in that restaurant and sobbed.

But I asked myself, Bill, who has a gun to your head? Who's forcing you to bite off more than you can chew? Who's intimidating you into overcommitting? Whose approval and affirmation and applause other than God's are you searching for that makes you live this way? The answers were worse than sobering. They were devastating.

The elders, to whom I'm accountable, did not cause my pace problem. Nor did the board or the staff or family or friends. The whole pace issue was a problem of my own making. I had no one else to blame. That's a terribly lonely feeling—having no one else to blame.

So I sat all alone in this cheap restaurant in South Haven, mad as a hornet that I couldn't blame anybody for my kingdom exhaustion and my emotional numbness. To find the bad guy, I had to look in a mirror.

To further complicate matters, the only person who can put a sustainability program together for your future is you. For fifteen years, I lived overcommitted and out of control, and deep down I kept saying, Why aren't the elders rescuing me? Why aren't my friends rescuing me? Don't people see I'm dying here?

But it isn't their job. It's my job. Please, if you haven't already, commit yourself to developing an approach to leadership that will enable you to endure over the long haul.

ARE MY GIFTS DEVELOPING?

Pop quiz: What are your top three spiritual gifts? If you cannot articulate them as quickly as you can give your name, address, and phone number, I'm tempted to say, "You need your cage rattled!" Before you write me a note telling me I've made you feel bad, I need to let you know that on this issue, I have Sympathy Deficit Disorder. Maybe I need medication or something. But seriously, leaders have to master their spiritual gift profile. They must know which gifts they've been given and how they rank in order.

In addition, the Bible holds every leader accountable before God for developing each of those gifts to the zenith of their spiritual potential.

It's sobering to have to ask myself regularly, Bill, you know God's only given you three gifts. Some people have five, six, or seven. You've been given three—leadership, evangelism, and teaching. Are you growing them? Developing, stretching these gifts? Reading everything you can read? Getting around people who are better than you in these areas? Are you developing the three gifts God has given you? Because those are the ones I've been given, they're the only ones I'm going to stand accountable for before God someday. I'm learning that I cannot give myself any slack when it comes to spiritual gift development.

IS MY HEART FOR GOD INCREASING AND MY CAPACITY FOR LOVING DEEPENING?

Have you reminded yourself recently whose job it is to grow your heart for God? Is it the church's job? Your small group's job? No. It's your job to make sure your heart for God is increasing. Nobody can do that for you. You've got to develop the spiritual practices that keep you growing toward Christlikeness.

Likewise, is your capacity for loving people deepening? If you think about it, you realize God has only one kind of treasure. It's people.

When our kids were young and Lynne and I needed some husband-wife time, we'd get a babysitter. And I'd give those sitters my little talk. As we were heading out, I would say, "You need to know something. We only have two treasures in this life, only two. I don't care if you wreck our car or if the house burns down while we're gone. Really. Just promise me. Promise me you'll take really good care of our children. They are all that really matter to us in this world." God is saying to leaders, "Promise me. Give me your word. Take care of my treasures. Grow in leadership so that you become the greatest you can be at taking care of my treasures. Love them. Nurture them. Develop them. Challenge them. Mature them. They are all that really matters to me in this world."

And right now would be a good time for you to say to God, "I will."

3

AVOIDING CULTURAL CONTAMINATION

———— ◉ ————

The Necessity of Purity in a Compromised World

MARK BUCHANAN

Jonah is my favorite prophet, and for no better reason than our uncanny resemblance. I'm bald and I figure him bald—why else his emotional tumult over how shade dappled or sun scorched his head? I'm short and I imagine him short: a stumpy, wiry guy, all that peevishness compacted tight as a nail bomb. He loved comfort and resented interruption, and that runs pretty close to my own bias. He was possessive, evasive, defensive, obsessive. Things not unknown to me.

Jonah is my least favorite prophet, and for exactly the same reason. He reminds me too much of me. I long to be Daniel-like in wisdom, Isaiah-like in righteousness, Ezekiel-like in faithfulness. I want the courage of Elijah, the endurance of Jeremiah, the long view of Zechariah. I dream of standing down kings and outrunning horses, commanding drought and deluge with a word, calling down woe like thunderbolts and blessing like manna.

But I'm plagued with Jonah-likeness.

And here's a deeper worry: so is the church. Not just my church, but *the* church—especially the church in North America. We're evasive with God, resentful toward outsiders, smug about our own goodness. Prudish, hawkish, lovers of comfort, and nursing a giant grudge against anyone and anything that threatens it.

Just like Jonah.

That's half the story, anyhow.

The other half is that the church is Esther, Esther prior to her awakening: assuming an insider status and willing to disguise her true identity for the sake of it, fearful of confronting her culture. We want to be like everyone else, only more so. We're a people terrified of being peculiar. We'll do almost anything to win a pagan king's affections.

Jonah wants just to be left alone, and would happily let everyone else go to hell. Esther wants just to fit in, and willingly forsakes her distinctiveness to achieve that. Between these two impulses, the kingdom always goes begging.

Jonah and, implicitly, his community, are threatened by Assyrian exile. Jonah is called as a missionary to the very people who bear that threat. Esther and, explicitly, her community, are in the clutches of Persian exile. Esther is called to take a stand against the very people in whose land she and her people dwell but who now threaten to destroy them.

Both stories are about God's people living amidst pagan culture—a culture that is pervasive, seductive, potentially coercive, and often at deep odds with what God thinks. Both are about the ways God's people try to negotiate their place toward or within that culture. And so both help us think through spiritual and ethical issues for such a time as this.

HOW THEN SHALL WE LIVE?

Jonah chooses the way of condemnation. He hates the culture that threatens his own. His attitude is leave us alone and be damned if you don't. He is prideful of his distinctiveness. "I am a Hebrew and

I worship the LORD, the God of heaven, who made the sea and the dry land," he smugly tells the sailors whose ship he's boarded, even though he's using these men to escape this God.[18] But he's not the least bit inclined to invite others to share in it.

So when God calls him to confront the people of Nineveh, Assyria's capital, for their wickedness, Jonah flees. He simply doesn't want to get involved. When God forces the issue, Jonah goes—grudgingly—and trumpets the doom of Nineveh, and then waits to behold it, and relish it. When the Ninevites repent and God shows mercy, Jonah throws a full-scale tantrum. This is what he long suspected God would do, and he turns surly and self-pitying about it.

Jonah's attitude toward pagan culture is an old standby for the church. Avoid outsiders, and when you can't, protest against them. Lament the sorry state of things. Call God's judgment down. Imagine, with pleasure, the punishment to be visited on the disobedient. Meanwhile, make yourself as comfortable as possible. And if the threatened divine judgment fails to materialize? Sulk. Mightily.

It's hard not to think here of some conservative churches' reaction to the homosexual community. I live in Canada, where recently our government, against the wishes of most Canadians, pushed through legislation that legalized same-sex marriage. A few months prior to that, I attended a citywide prayer meeting where this issue was at the forefront. Emotions were strong. I expected that, but what caught me by surprise was the tone of the meeting. It had a Jonah-like ring: jingoistic, gloating, self-righteous. People warmed quickly to themes of divine vengeance. They evoked it in vivid imagery.

The problem here is tactical as well as spiritual. Spiritually, we should be careful what we eat. Bloodthirst causes heartburn, severely. But tactically, this is hardly a way to start a kingdom revolution. The church, on this issue, should be begging God to help us be Mark 2 communities: when people find out Jesus is in the house, they're willing to break the roof open if that's what it takes to get themselves and their sick friends inside.

I have talked with gay people about how they see Christians. Generally they see us as, well, you know the drill: bigoted, angry, narrow, hateful, afraid—it's a caricature, I know. Only, everything about that citywide prayer meeting supported it.

What if God's larger desire is to invite people, all people, into the wideness of his mercy? Somehow the Ninevites were able to respond to God despite Jonah's rancor and belligerence. After all, judgment is real, not to be trifled with. God's wrath is being revealed against all godlessness and wickedness.

Only Jonah doesn't know anything but judgment. He is a Johnny-one-note. In God's kingdom, judgment entwines with invitation, and is usually uttered with deep heartache ("Oh, Jerusalem, Jerusalem . . ."). It's God's kindness that leads to repentance. That kindness needs to be visible in the church. The consummation of the church's missionary role will be that day when ten people from every tribe and tongue—Nineveh included—take hold of the hem of the robe of one believer and say, "Let us go with you, for we have heard that God is with you."[19]

But Jonah is not interested. He doesn't want his enemy's repentance. He doesn't want them in church, singing the songs of Zion. He certainly doesn't want them coming to his church and bringing their own strange music with them. He wants them to pay, to suffer. He wants judgment, not mercy.

Jonah's moral dogmatism, I think, hides his theological ambivalence. That's usually what dogmatism does. Jonah is wary and begrudging, not just toward Ninevites, but toward God. He's boastful of his knowledge of God but cagey in his relationship with him. He finds God both too hard and too soft—hard toward his chosen ones, soft toward the enemy. God, in his view, lacks an appropriate sense of favoritism.

I wonder if this isn't the hidden motive of churches that take up Jonah's style. Maybe the angry, accusatory stance is mostly a mask for our own misgivings about God.

"Fanaticism is overcompensation for doubt," said the late Canadian novelist. We can trace this theological trajectory in the Pharisees. They disapproved of whatever they did not initiate. But Jesus identified their problem as a broken relationship with God. They overcompensated for doubt.

CONDEMNATION OR ABSORPTION?

Jonah wants to condemn the culture. He would love to see it destroyed. The idea that it could be reclaimed, redeemed, invited to share in the goodness of God—such thinking is anathema to him. After all, he can hardly invite anyone, friend or foe, to taste and see that the Lord is good when he has not tasted and seen such things himself.

That's only half our problem. The other half is being Esther, prior to her moment of reckoning. When it comes to pagan culture, Esther moves in precisely the opposite direction.

Jonah avoids it, caricatures it, condemns it. Esther accepts it, embraces it, extols it.

Many early interpreters and Bible commentators viewed Esther (and/or the Jewish community depicted in the book) as a type of the church in compromised, semi-pagan form. Modern interpreters generally dismiss typological readings of Scripture (with good reason), but as one who adjusts to a hostile culture, her example can be instructive.

She conforms to whatever standards the culture sets—dress like the reigning pop queen, subscribe to whatever attitudes are *au courant*—in order to look like everyone else, only better.

And here, it's hard not to think of many mainline churches. In the recent controversy over same-sex marriage in Canada, entire denominations have aligned themselves with the spirit of the age. They want to be deemed beautiful in the eyes of the pagan king. The Anglican Church in Canada is even ostracizing dissenting churches and defrocking their ministers. The idea that the church should do anything other than endorse the culture's current thinking on sexual matters is, in the minds of these denominational leaders, a throwback to medievalism. We're in a new millennium now, is the rallying cry. We must move with the times.

If Jonah's theological ilk were the Pharisees, Esther's were the Sadducees. They valued expedience above faithfulness (or, more to the point, equated the two). The worst sin was to be out of kilter with the culture's dominant values. Their highest goal was to reduce the lag time between the latest trends and their blessing thereof.

Of course, Esther eventually awakens from this. She realizes, in the nick of time, that the culture whose acceptance she craves is laying ambush for her and her people. And then, with savvy and courage, she finds a new way of living in exile.

But before that happens, Esther immerses herself in pagan culture. The idea that she should confront it, or refuse its wares, is unthinkable. She wants to be left alone too—not by the culture, but by any sense that her primary loyalty lies elsewhere.

Jonah and Esther define two of the church's reactions to today's values.

Shun and denounce.

Embrace and extol.

In my own church, I see both attitudes. Recently, I made a comment from the pulpit that the starting place for Christians to uphold the "sanctity of marriage" is not the courts but our own households.

I cited statistics on divorce rates among evangelical Christians that put us pretty much in a dead heat with society at large. I talked about the high incidence of spousal abuse within conservative churches. I spoke about the widespread estrangement that prevails among many church-going couples. I mentioned the hidden plague of Internet porn that is withering intimacy between husbands and wives.

Some people came out swinging: stop meddling with matters in here, they told me. Start condemning what's happening out there.

Jonah.

On the other side, the statistics on premarital sex among evangelicals hardly distinguish us from all the other people on the face of the earth. And yet whenever I address this, a few folks take me aside and say, in effect, what's the big deal? Aren't there more important issues? A few kids are mixing it up between the sheets—well, so? Why fuss over that when we have a crisis of global warming, when the Amazonian rainforests are disappearing, when the sperm whale faces extinction? Recently, the Christian parents of a girl from our church tried to convince her to go on the pill. She sat them down and told them in no uncertain terms that she had no intention of having sex until she was married. They told her that was unrealistic, and she should go on it anyhow.

Esther.

MORALITY OR PURITY?

What's the alternative? I think Daniel is our best guide for such a time as this. He stands between the extremes of Esther and Jonah. He, like Esther, lived in a time of exile—Babylonian, then Persian. He lived among people mostly indifferent to his own convictions but who, when put off by those convictions, grew swiftly and menacingly hostile. He had to sort out his place within that culture: what could he, without violating conscience, say yes to? What must he, regardless of the personal risk, say no to?

Daniel had neither Jonah's surly, haughty ways nor Esther's coy, accommodating manner. He had simple clarity and quiet integrity. Some things about the pagan culture—their education system, the political structure, their habit of naming you after one of their gods—no problem. Go to their schools. Work in their government. Bear their god's name.

But one thing especially was taboo: king's food. Of that Daniel would not partake. The food wasn't wrong in and of itself. But it had been dedicated to pagan deities. To partake was to submit. To eat was to worship. So better to subsist on a diet of raw vegetables than eat the king's rich meats and richer sauces, his wines and confections.

But Daniel and his companions did not merely subsist on vegetables: they thrived. They ended up more healthy and bright-eyed than all the other young men being trained with them.

We can sit under the teaching of our culture and emerge shrewder in our own convictions. We can participate in the government of our culture and bring glory to God by our diligence and integrity. We can be named after our culture's deities (Mark—god of war!) and not suffer diminishment to our faith.

What we can't do is eat king's food.

But what is king's food now? What is that element within our culture that, if the people of God participate in it, will ruin us?

I think it's our culture's sexual ethics.

What this culture lacks is purity. The church—especially Jonah—has not helped here much, because always we want to impose morality. Purity is to morality what intimacy is to acquaintance, what love is to tolerance, what oneness is to equality. Purity is not just a higher thing: it is a category unto itself.

I think we should stop preaching morality and start preaching purity. After all, no one wants to drink merely sterilized water, chlorinated water, water with a drop of iodine.

What awakens and then slakes thirst is pure water.

Daniel embraces the way of purity. He will not taint his body with what has been dedicated to another god. And if there's a clear lesson from his story, it's this: that is the one true way to win a pagan king's heart. Everywhere Daniel goes, the king ends up acknowledging that God alone is God.

At our church, we call young people to the way of purity, not morality. We call them to be Daniels. Far from languishing, they thrive.

Not long ago, I was invited by an Esther-like church to do a one-day seminar on worship. I was surprised by the invitation—I don't get many like it. The pastor who invited me told me that most of his colleagues were deeply wary of me, some openly hostile. He told me of one fellow pastor who phoned him to denounce me. He denounced evangelicals as a breed. "What has this man in common with us?" he demanded to know.

"Why don't you come and see?" the host pastor replied.

I came with a team of worship leaders and dancers, men and women in their late teens or early twenties. Only a handful of people had registered. Even in the church's tiny sanctuary, they seemed thinly scattered. I kept watching for the man who hated me. Though I had never met him, I knew him the moment he entered. He walked in like he was hunting vermin. He sat down, his arms locked across his chest. When we started singing and asked the people to stand, he remained seated. He scrutinized the words on the overhead.

After lunch, we led seminars. The dancers taught basic choreography. The musicians taught basic song writing. And I taught a basic theology of worship. The man came to mine. He sat beside me, spoiling for a fight.

Ten minutes into it, he erupted. A woman commented how the mainline church had compromised the gospel, and he started trading blows with her. He had a litany of evangelical crimes against humanity. The argument escalated, and the host pastor jumped in.

"Well," he said, mild mannered. "I think the mainline tradition is perhaps somewhat narrow in its ecclesiology and broadly tolerant in its theology. Whereas the evangelical tradition is rigidly narrow in its theology, and somewhat loosey-goosey in its ecclesiology."

A brief moment of silence followed. I seized my opportunity. "Who here are pastors?" I asked. A few put up their hands, including the angry man.

"Let me ask you this," I said. "The young people I brought today, do you like them?"

Everyone did, including the angry man.

"Are there many young people like that in your own churches, who are that passionate, that in love with God, that committed to the church and her mission?"

No, they all said.

"Do you want young people like these in your churches?"

Yes, they all said.

"With all due respect," I said. "I think you don't have them exactly because of your broadly tolerant theology. That theology helped abort a third of their peers. With all due respect, it assisted in creating a sexual ethic that robbed this generation of intimacy and hope. It has driven most of them out of the church.

"My opinion? If you're really serious about seeing this kind of young people in your churches—not just warming the pews but leading—you might consider being less broadly tolerant."

I went on to speak about how we don't teach our young people to be moral. We teach them to be pure. We call them to be Daniels.

"You can see for yourself," I said, "the difference that makes."

I looked over at the man who hated me. He was stricken. I thought he hated me even more. I thought he would walk out. But to my surprise, he came back for the last session.

To my delight, he stood when we sang. To my amazement, he opened his arms and held them like he was catching rain.

And he sang with gusto. "Great is thy faithfulness," he declared. I think he meant it.

Daniel tends to have that effect on people.

4

THE FALL

———— ◉ ————

Don't Wait for a Near-Fatal Climbing Accident before
Reconsidering Your Approach to Life

NATHAN CONRAD
AS TOLD TO MATT WOODLEY

It looked like another perfect day for ice climbing—sunny, twenty-five degrees, with a light snow and a calm breeze. On Monday our party of four climbers had already climbed some smaller cliffs. After a year off from climbing, we needed to start on these easier, more familiar routes. Now on Tuesday, February 8, 2011, as we looked over the dozen or so climbs in the area, we decided to try something more challenging—like "Dracula," a well-known route that's part of Frankenstein Cliffs in Crawford Notch, New Hampshire.

Although Dracula is ranked one and a half to two grades beyond any climb I'd ever led, I was excited to stretch my skills. I've always enjoyed ice climbing. I relish the sport's personal challenge and physical demands, but I also appreciate the teamwork and camaraderie. So on Tuesday, as I went with three other experienced climbers to the base of Dracula, I felt ready to lead. Another friend would climb as the "second," a team member who follows the leader and cleans up the pieces of gear left on the ice.

Many people assume that climbing is risky and reckless. Veteran climber Jon Krakauer admits that the sport is "wrapped in tales of audacity and danger"—and sometimes for good reason. But climbers also know they can drastically minimize the risks by working out before the climb and then by using safety techniques while on the climb. As I started to climb Dracula, I felt comfortable with both my conditioning and my climbing abilities.

But about two-thirds of the way up the 110-foot wall, the climb started to unravel. By this point I had already placed two pieces of protection into the ice. These "ice screws" serve as safety anchors that catch a climber if he falls. I considered placing a third ice screw, but I decided to push myself a little more and climb a little higher. Somewhere during this push fatigue caught up with me. About thirty to thirty-five feet above my last screw, I could feel my muscles beginning to fail. It suddenly hit me that I might not be able to finish the climb—or even have the strength to put in another screw for protection.

My arms and legs started to shake. Fear swept over me as I thought, *I am going to fall!*

In desperation, I set my axes as deep as I could, kicked my boots into the ice, and called out for a rescue from one of my climbing partners. He grabbed a carabiner (a metal loop) and tossed it up to me. Now I just needed to hook into the rope—to prevent a fall.

But my body wouldn't cooperate. On my first attempt, I didn't grab enough of my own rope to clip the rescue line. As I tried the move again, suddenly everything gave out. My footholds blew out, the axes popped off, and I felt myself plunging. I plummeted seventy feet, crashing into an angled ice shelf and bouncing away from the ice. Then the rope went taut and swung me back to the cliff.

Amazingly, I was conscious, and as I dangled from my rope, my initial fear was that I might fall farther. Desperately I tried to grab my climbing axes (which are normally on leashes attached to my wrists) so I could stop another fall. I knew my body was injured, but I didn't know how badly. I didn't feel much except shock that I had fallen that far. I'd lost my footing before, but I'd never experienced a fall. I kept thinking, *I can't believe that I just fell. I* can't *believe that happened to me.*

After the fall, one of my climbing friends said, "That was the scariest thing I've ever seen in my life." But immediately after the fall, they sprang into action. One gently but firmly told me, "Nate, we got you. You're secure. We're going to let you down now." When I heard those words, I finally stopped struggling and let them take charge.

As I was lowered to the base of Dracula, in demonstration of God's grace, two strangers were standing there, and one of them identified himself as an ER doctor. He examined me and said, "You're going to be okay, but we need to get you to a hospital." But the nearest vehicle was a mile and a half away.

So after the doctor examined me, we glissaded (slid) down the snowy approach, and with my climbing buddies alongside, I slowly trudged the mile and a half to the van. As we drove to the nearest hospital, my fears increased. Blood was coming out of a wound in my forehead, and my nose was bleeding. I started to lose vision in one eye.

But we made it to the hospital, and after three days of treatment and observation the doctors released me. Overall, mine were fairly minor injuries: a fractured fibula, a fractured pinkie, along with cranial and orbital fractures behind my eye.

"FALLOUT" FROM THE FALL

But the physical damage wasn't the worst part of the fall. It would take much longer to recover from the spiritual, relational, and emotional impact of what happened over the next few months.

One of my climbing buddies had recorded our last three annual trips. So this climb—with all my climbing mistakes—had also been recorded on video. After the accident, he did some interviews with the ER doctor and a climbing guide, shaped it into a fourteen-minute video, and then decided to share the video on Vimeo (an amateur videographer site).[20]

None of us anticipated the attention the video would get. All around the country, other climbers viewed, shared, dissected, and even ridiculed my climbing mistakes. I quickly became the poster child for how not to climb on ice.

Will Gadd, America's foremost authority on climbing, watched the video and posted it to his blog, offering a helpful but brutally honest critique of my climb. In a series of two lengthy posts (one of them titled "How Not to Suck"), Gadd told the climbing community that I had "absolutely no business being on lead on ice." He called my footwork "terrible" and he was amazed I hadn't fallen earlier. Gadd concluded his first post by telling his readers that I should say to myself, "Only through incredible luck did I not completely [mess] myself up for the rest of my life; I need to rethink my approach to ice climbing."

Those words ripped deep into my soul, especially since I consider myself an avid climber. But I knew Gadd was right—actually, he was even more right than he realized. After his blog post, I sent Gadd a personal e-mail. "This isn't just about climbing," I confessed, "it's about my whole approach to life." In other words, this experience seemed to epitomize the brokenness in my own soul, my attachment to life-sucking idols like control and approval, and the unhealthy habits ingrained in my approach to life, relationships, and ministry.

I'm discovering that the mistakes, the patterns, and even the "sins" of my climbing technique were equally evident in my approach to everything I do. I don't have all the answers at this point, but the accident has forced me to ask some soul-searching questions about relationships and my walk with Christ.

AM I ADMITTING MY LIMITS?

When the video made the rounds in the climbing community, fellow climbers pointed out the obvious: this guy was in over his head. For some reason, I couldn't make that assessment about myself. My gut may have told me that climbing lead on Dracula exceeded my abilities, but in the thrill of doing something new and challenging, I brushed those feelings aside.

Climbers call this "getting into a pump," a massive adrenaline rush that clouds your judgment as you charge up the route. When a climber gets "super pumped," adrenaline trumps everything else—fatigue, safety, and even common sense. So while the adrenaline flooded my brain with a sense of invincibility, my muscles started to shut down.

At that point, I should have opted to (1) stop, place an ice screw, and rest; or (2) rappel off and call it a partial climb. Instead, hyped-up on adrenaline, I kept charging up Dracula's treacherous wall of ice.

In the process I kept rationalizing my position: *I feel okay; I'll rest at the next break; I've got enough in me to finish this climb; I can't stop here (or at all) because I need to keep moving.* The truth should have been obvious: I was climbing well past my protection, in a weakened condition, and ignorant of resting and safety measures. That's why more experienced climbers know that you just can't get super pumped on a climb; the consequences of getting exhausted and overextended are too great.

Since the accident, I've started to assess how my climbing patterns repeat themselves in the rest of my life. In many ways, I've lived my whole life—including my approach to ministry—by blithely ignoring or intentionally rebelling against God-given limits. As a result, I have a simple strategy for dealing with the fatigue and pain of ministry: suck it up and keep going. And if work gets more difficult, I just put my head down and work even harder.

Thankfully, I'm now learning that there's a healthier approach to life and ministry. In his book *The Emotionally Healthy Church*, pastor Peter Scazzero contends that "embracing our God-given limits is at the core of our calling . . . as spiritual leaders"—and that's especially true in our frantic, busy, driven church cultures. "When we don't respect God's limits in our lives," Scazzero writes, "we will often find ourselves overextended, stressed and exhausted."[21]

The accident has helped me untangle the deep roots underneath this tendency. Namely, I often resent limits because I'm driven by idols of achievement and approval. I need people to see me as the good pastor, the smooth preacher, and the tender-hearted shepherd who is available to everyone. This was what drove my seventy-five-hour work weeks. This was what left my soul empty, my body exhausted, and my relationships frayed. Sadly, this driven approach to ministry doesn't just hurt me; it also puts others at risk. I'm beginning to see when I get into a pastoral super pump, I can easily disconnect from God, neglect my wife and kids, and fail to be present to the people I lead in the church.

This isn't just about climbing . . . This experience seemed to epitomize the brokenness in my own soul.

Nearly a year after the fall, I'm better at regularly asking myself some honest questions: When do I get into a super pump? Am I exceeding my God-given limits? Have I confused the zeal needed to serve God, grow a church, and start new programs with a surge of high-powered hormones? In other words, is this about God or me? Am I being led by the Holy Spirit or by my own adrenaline?

Naturally, I haven't changed overnight. I'm still identifying the idols that can drive my approach to ministry. But I'm learning that leadership also involves respecting limits. For instance, I'm accepting the fact that my body and soul can only handle so many hours of work in a typical week. I'm adjusting to the reality that my wife and kids can only thrive under a certain pace. Church members can only grow so fast. A consistent pattern of violating these limits may not always lead to an immediate and tragic fall, but why would I want to force myself or others to climb beyond God's protective limits? These limits aren't barriers to one's work; they're gifts that breathe life into it.

WHO IS SPEAKING INTO MY LIFE?

After the fall, I suddenly became hungry for advice. Hearing the critiques from Will Gadd and others motivated me to connect with more experienced climbers. I read their blogs and wrote e-mails asking for more information. I ordered and read books. I replayed the advice from the climbing guide at the scene of my accident.

Like anything else, ice climbing has a body of knowledge and a skill base. It requires mentoring and learning, instruction and practice. For climbers, that means humbly and patiently learning about knots and ropes, rest methods, safety checks and double checks, footwork, self-arrest and self-belay methods, screw placements, route selection, and equipment inspection for overuse and damage.

It's a steep learning curve. Somebody has to teach me this stuff, while I stay humble enough to learn the skills and develop as a climber.

Fortunately, in the midst of the public ridicule, I found an unlikely climbing mentor—my initial critic, Will Gadd. After his first blog posts, he sent me a few personal e-mails and offered some practical advice. First, he told me to practice with top-rope climbs—a simple skill that involves tying a rope to a tree and throwing it down a cliff. It's a safe way to practice techniques without climbing past your protection. Then Gadd bluntly told me to find an experienced climber and ask him to train me, even if it cost money. In his words, "The money spent for a good day of instruction is [much] cheaper than a broken leg, skull fracture, or death."

Finally, Gadd offered some encouragement: "I'm stoked to help in any way I can, and never take anything you read on the Internet too seriously. Chin up, learn from the valid points, but do not submit to the haters. Drink coffee in a dark basement—or whatever it takes to process all of this . . . . As you've noted, the question is what to do with all of this. I'm invested in this too, so let's have some fun and get better."

That was also what I needed to hear about pastoring: don't do ministry alone, find a mentor, and let others speak into your life. Find someone with more ministry experience who can transfer pastoral skills, point out your blind spots, and offer constructive feedback. It might take time and money, but it's better than the alternative: a ministry breakdown or a personal blowout.

So I've started asking questions like: Who has the right to speak into my life? Who knows my sins, weaknesses, and bad habits and then has the love and courage to confront me? Do I even welcome that sort of "push back" in my relationships? I'm now learning to seek out these kinds of relationships—relationships based on fierce honesty, tender trust, and committed love. And relationships like this don't just benefit me. I'm also learning how important it is for me to model an approachable, welcoming, God-dependent style of life and leadership, rather than an arrogant, invulnerable, and self-sufficient style.

I'm starting to allow—and even to seek out—critiques about my patterns, my sins, and needed growth areas. At one point, during a weeklong conference that focused on spiritual renewal, a conversation with my wife and our discipler revealed a deep pool of anger within me. My anger came from my need to control and please other people. As a result, I placed enormous expectations on my wife, the church, and myself, and when I didn't measure up, it stoked my anger.

My wife quietly but courageously described my impatience, workaholism, hardness of heart, and harsh words. I was wounding her spirit. At first I bristled with anger, but the words slowly pierced my pride and softened my hard heart. Of course it still hurts to hear the truth about my faults—whether it's from my wife or the climbing community. But since the accident I've gained a new appreciation for the opportunity to grow through honest feedback.

WILL I LEARN FROM MY FAILURES?

Lots of people in the climbing community make mistakes. Every year people fall, get hurt, and even die—sometimes because of avoidable mistakes. But thanks to the video and the Internet, my mistakes had been captured and spread around the world. Rarely have people been able to watch a fall like this, and see the errors of a climber so clearly. The video is not a trailer of total incompetence, but there rarely exists in the climbing community a video of what not to do, and a lively forum to dissect and learn from the accident.

The reaction in climbing circles was quick, intense, and harsh. Comments posted included: "Total ignorance." "SELL all your gear." "I don't think this cat has many lives left."

Like most leaders, I value my reputation. I want people to think that I'm competent and capable. So the more people viewed and dissected the video, the more I felt embarrassed and ashamed. One guy even posted on Will Gadd's blog: "If I were this guy, I'd never show my face in New Hampshire again." I agreed with him. I wanted to hide—or at least I desperately wanted to spin the story so I didn't look that bad.

My fallen, insecure heart dreads the exposure that comes through failure. I want others to see my successes—not my flops.

Of course this aversion to failure can thwart courageous leadership. As Seth Godin said at a recent Leadership Summit, "If failure is not an option, then neither is success." So once again, the fall forced me to question my assumptions. How do I respond to failure? Does it make me run and hide? If not, why do I respond with fear and shame? Do I consistently identify and learn from my failures? Do those I lead view me as a model for how to fail with grace and humility? Do I respond well to others when they fail?

WHO'S THE REAL HERO HERE?

For most of my ministry, I've believed in what I'll call "the mythic pastor-as-ultimate-hero story." My fallen heart has often craved this version of the leadership story. It's a story that puts me at the center. I must be the ever-competent, invincible, irrepressible, and even righteous (or semi-righteous, or at least more righteous than most people) spiritual leader who can serve God heroically, without making mistakes—at least noticeable ones.

Once I buy into the pastor-as-ultimate-hero story I'm trapped. I remain stuck in my unhealthy patterns and sinful desires: I remain a slave to the fears of failure and disapproval. I work harder and ignore the work of the Spirit. I don't depend on God because I want to be the hero of the story. But if God can humble me, helping me to admit my mistakes, confess my failures, and embrace my limits, then he alone receives the worship and praise for the story of my life.

When God is the hero of the story, when he is the director, producer, narrator, and star, then my failures don't imply automatic defeat because they point people to his greatness, not mine. My failures don't end the story, because ultimately the story isn't about me.

Since the fall, I've become more open to admitting my failures. The accident exposed my resistance to have Jesus at center stage. Stories like this, showing my failings and his grace, become a far better narrative for life and ministry.

God is the hero, not me. I don't have to top out, prove myself, work through a pump, or push past my limitations in order to prove something to myself or anyone else. We've all got opportunities to talk about God's provision. Sometimes those moments are a little more humiliating than others.

For the sake of the Kingdom, we are invited, like the disciples, to tell the story of our ignorance, stubbornness, and failings—but we can also tell the story of how God's grace triumphs over our sin.

PART II

NECESSARY REPAIRS

Putting a Band-Aid over the caution light on your car's instrument panel will accomplish two things: one positive, one negative. On the positive side, it will shield a potential problem and financial headache from your view, removing a source of irritation, distraction, and worry. (If, in fact, you can really look at that Band-Aid every day without remembering what it covers.) On the not-so-positive side of the ledger, you may miss an opportunity to keep your car in operation, leaving you stranded, perhaps, on some desolate roadside after dark.

We can close our eyes to needed maintenance in our spiritual lives, as well. The witness of Scripture, the still, small voice of the Holy Spirit, and the counsel of a spouse or trusted friend may point to areas in our lives that really need to be addressed—attitudes, habits, deepening ruts, or even addictions.

God will certainly restore and renew us, if we humbly seek his help. But we must first be willing to admit that our lives are in need of repair. If we don't, we may find ourselves like the Laodiceans who plugged their ears, closed their eyes, and in the midst of bankruptcy kept exclaiming, "I am rich; I have acquired wealth and do not need a thing."[22]

When you think about it, denial has looked pretty much the same for the last two thousand years.

In this section we'll find timely help from Francis Chan, Bill Hybels, Eugene Peterson, and Steve May, who will point us toward truth that will alert us to danger—and equip us for the long haul.

5

TUNING YOUR ENGINE

———— ◉ ————

*Pursue Spiritual Formation and Allow
the Holy Spirit to Do His Work*

FRANCIS CHAN

When I preach, I want my sermons to form people's spiritual commitment in two ways: First, I want them to hear what God is teaching me through his Word. I want them to understand what a passage means. Second, I also want to be open to what the Holy Spirit wants to do in that moment. So my sermons aren't as scripted as they used to be.

I made this shift because I want to be as real as possible, and if I script too much, especially with four services, it can become mechanical—just going through motions rather than really depending on God in the moment. I also want to be open to the fact that there are different crowds in each service, and when I open my mouth the Spirit might give me different words to say to each group. If I have a script, I tend to stick to it even if God may be leading me elsewhere in the moment.

This wrestling with the role of the Holy Spirit has been a gradual thing over several years. For several years in my ministry, I really operated as though the Holy Spirit didn't exist. The truth is I trusted in the flesh—the natural abilities that God gave me—the same way unbelievers trust their natural gifts. With my natural communication abilities, I could probably gather a crowd even without the Spirit. But I realized in the church there's got to be something more beyond what I can do through my own talents. There's got to be something supernatural, something only the Holy Spirit can do.

I study the Bible because it comes from God and there is supernatural power in the gospel and in his written Word. But I'm less convinced that sitting down for hours and crafting the perfect sermon is what it's about. I'd rather study the Scriptures and live such a life that when I pray or speak, the Spirit gives me what he wants me to say. As I've seen God be faithful with that, I want more and more of it in my ministry.

This new dependence on the Holy Spirit started when a few of our leaders began studying the role of elders in the Scriptures. "You know," they said, "our elder meetings are more like business meetings. We discuss how much we should pay to repave the parking lot. But in the Bible the role of elders has more to do with shepherding, teaching, and prayer." So we made a shift. We had the staff do more of the business work, and the elders started studying the Scriptures to see where the Lord wanted to lead the church spiritually.

Our elder meetings began to include a lot more discussion of theology, Scripture, and discipleship. We began to realize that, in our church, we were missing some of the obvious teachings of Scripture. And we started questioning the values we'd gotten from our culture.

Our American culture is all about shallow relationships. Facebook and Twitter are the quintessential examples. We have a lot of "friends," but we know very few of them on a meaningful level. We need to start looking each other in the eye and having deeper, more meaningful, face-to-face connections and conversations. We realized we'd rather have ten solid relationships in the church than ten thousand shallow ones.

Another reason for our shallow relationships is that our culture tells us we should be completely independent or else rely on the government and insurance to protect us. But within the church, God wants us to be interdependent. We are directed to care for one another, look out for one another, and we are to be each other's security. So we made a commitment among the elders that if anything were to happen to any of us, we would take care of one another's families.

As a culture, we're so worried about what's going to happen to us thirty years from now that we are not taking care of our brothers and sisters who need help today. Jesus tells us not to worry about tomorrow, let alone thirty years down the line.

I'm trying to picture the gathering where somebody says, "Why don't we get rid of our insurance and promise to share everything?" You may wonder, when our elders made that commitment to each other, did any of them hesitate and say "I'm with you in theory, but I'm not quite ready to do it"? No, with that group there wasn't a lot of hesitation, which was surprising. We had been talking about this sort of thing for a long time, and they had been thinking it through in their own times with the Lord. The fact that our elders have been together for years helped to ease the decision. We have a close relationship. There is trust.

That trust is the critical component to this kind of transformation among leaders. The reason why an elder could look at me and say, "Francis, I promise if anything happens to you, I will take care of your family," and the reason I believed him, is because I've lived life with him. I've seen these elders' convictions before the Lord, and I know they're not just empty words. So there's trust there, and I think that's the way it ought to be. There are a lot of churches with leaders that aren't living out their faith together. Instead they're trying to bring transformation by creating programs. It won't work.

Because we have shifted our focus from self-reliance to mutual reliance through the power of the Holy Spirit, spiritual formation of our people does not rest on me alone. When we took this step, we realized that a church our size should have fifty or sixty elders, and we began the process of training many more. We had neglected that under the old model because we thought it would be impossible to make a decision with sixty people in a room. It's hard enough with ten. But then we realized we were talking about two different things—shepherding and decision making. We appointed more elders to shepherd the congregation, but much of the decision making is reserved for a smaller team—six or eight of us.

We've seen these changes trickle out to the rest of the community. After making that commitment of mutual dependence, we began sharing our possessions more as elders. Soon we had begun to expand the practice to share with those we are close to—people in our neighborhoods and others in the church. And the circle continued to expand. Now people in the church are giving away their cars, writing checks to those in need, sharing their possessions, and even their houses. It is an inevitable principle: everything rises and falls with leadership. We teach by our example.

The example of the elders and leadership is more important, even in a large church, than having the right programs or preaching. There are many churches with leaders who aren't living out their faith together, and they don't have trust. That's why they try to bring transformation by creating programs. That's why you often hear of people who say, "I love church but once I got into the leadership, the inner workings, I was so disillusioned." The example did not match the teaching. That's a terrible indictment.

In a recent book I wrote, "I cannot convince people to be obsessed with Jesus, and that's why you need the Holy Spirit." By that I mean it takes more than good preaching to make authentic disciples. Once you pastor for a while, it dawns on you that nailing a sermon doesn't mean lives will be transformed. Or you'll meet a person who's surrendered everything to Christ, and you'll realize that nothing you preached and nothing you did caused him to become a believer.

One day a man who had been in our church for fifteen years told me that my preaching hadn't changed him. He said I spoke too much about the "narrow road" and how everyone needs to be radical for Christ. He said there's also a "middle road" where people like him can do a lot of good things. I was floored by that. He's sat under my teaching for fifteen years, and he still believes there isn't only a wide, easy road and a narrow, difficult road, but also a middle road? I've been told many times that my teaching is really helpful, that I make things simple for people to understand. And then you hear something like that and it all crumbles into dust.

That's when I remember, I cannot make someone fall in love with Jesus. I do not transform people; God does.

This really came home for me, literally, with my own teenage daughter when she told me that she was not in love with Jesus. I spent nights crying, bawling, and praying to the Lord. Here I am known for my ability to communicate, but there was nothing I could do for my own daughter that would make her fall in love with Jesus. Of course I could still guide and lead her, but I was powerless to convict her.

I prayed, "God, either your Spirit comes into her or your Spirit doesn't. It doesn't matter how great a dad I am. I cannot bring her to life."

Then one day she came into my room and said, "You were right, Dad. The Holy Spirit was not in me. But now he is." She talked about how near she was to God and how everything had changed. My wife and I were skeptical. We wanted to see evidence of change. But months later, I can say she really is a new creation. I didn't do that. It was the Holy Spirit.

I've got to quit trying to play the Holy Spirit's role by forcing, manipulating, talking, and programming people into the change I want to see. Instead I've got to spend more time praying that the Holy Spirit would come into their lives and regenerate them.

So what's the point of all the work, sermon prep, and programs if the outcome is out of our hands? Some of our toil is wasted, because we're toiling in the belief that these things do change people. But the experiences I related above have shown me that a lot more of our work needs to be put into prayer, study of the Word, and trusting God. I could spend an extra ten hours on every sermon, trying to get every word just right, but my time would be much better spent sharing the gospel with people and praying.

Don't misunderstand me; I do study hard, because the Scripture tells me to and because I want to be accurate in my teaching. We should work hard "as unto the Lord," but we have to let our theology guide what we work hard at. And we have to be led by the Spirit as to how much time to spend crafting a sermon and how much time to spend praying for a movement of the Spirit.

Churches that are built through our effort rather than the Spirit's will quickly collapse when we stop pushing and prodding people along. Of course, we should push, prod, and persuade men and women to love Christ and put their trust in the Holy Spirit, but not to do more, try harder, or get involved in more programs. I've learned to spend a lot more time praying and asking the Spirit to move and begging God to send forth laborers. The more you look at Scripture, the more you realize that nothing happens unless God is behind it. *Jesus* is building *his* church. I just want to be a part of that. I'll keep doing my work, but the fruit is up to him. We can only pray, "Please, please, please let us see your Spirit at work. May it be like a mighty wind that moves us."

Let me illustrate this dependence on the Holy Spirit with an example from surfing. Sometimes I'm out in the ocean and there are no sets coming in. I really don't want to paddle in, so I pray, "God, give me one nice set, one good wave to take me back to shore." I pray because I can't make a wave, and I can't ask my friends to go further out and splash to create a wave. We're powerless. That's what I think often happens in church and in life. We think we can make waves, but in reality we're totally dependent on the Spirit.

I happen to be a pastor of a megachurch. A large gathering where everyone is singing really loud is nice, but it's not an indication that the Spirit is at work. If enthusiastic music indicated success, then we'd be spending more money on better musicians and better worship leaders. But that's not how our elder board measures success. Nor is it how God measures it.

In God's eyes, success is people loving each other deeply, caring for one another, digging deep in each other's lives, sharing their possessions, and sharing the gospel in their communities. Are they fully devoted followers of Jesus? Is transformation happening? Do they see themselves as part of something bigger than themselves—a body with a mission larger than the individual? Our job is not to get as many people into church as possible. Our job is to make sure that we're setting a biblical pattern.

When we were debating between launching video venues or moving me back and forth between worship services, one of the elders challenged me by asking, "Don't you want to create a reproducible model? Isn't that what we see in Scripture and isn't that the only thing that would satisfy you—a movement that goes beyond the limitations of a wall?" He was absolutely right—it is more biblical to entrust leadership to other shepherds rather than put everything on one person. That's when our church decided to put more focus on home gatherings.

The groups are intentionally geographically based. We felt that even in church, people will find likeminded people with the same interests, and that's not biblical. We are called to love people who are completely different from ourselves. Think Philemon and Onesemus. And we really believe if you've got a sister in Christ living next door, God wants you to know her and love her even if she's completely different from you. That's the beauty of the body of Christ, and we want to paint that picture in our neighborhoods.

We've positioned elders in different neighborhoods to be shepherds of these groups, and we're developing elders in neighborhoods where we don't yet have any groups. And other leaders have said they'd be willing to move to go wherever there isn't an elder to lead.

We do not require the elders to do all the teaching in these home groups. We want them to spend their time shepherding the people, really loving them and caring for them. As volunteers, it's hard for them to spend ten or fifteen hours a week preparing a message. So we prepare a DVD with me sitting on a couch doing some teaching. But we only provide the video twice each month. We also want our elders to learn how to teach, so at least once a month they will do the teaching for the group. And in time they may not need the DVDs anymore.

Now that home gatherings are our new focus, keeping the large Sunday worship service going can be a distraction. But I'm committed to it for now. The people in the home gatherings love them. Some have said they'll never go back to the old way of church, but others just don't get it yet. And to be fair to them, I've taught one model of church for so many years that I can't expect them to jump to a completely new model at the drop of a hat. So for now I look at these Sunday services as a transition time for me to shepherd and patiently help funnel people into these smaller gatherings.

Maybe someday we won't have the large gatherings. For now, it doesn't make any sense to end them. But some day it might. Sometimes I wonder if God wants to use Cornerstone as an example of how to decentralize the church and empower other leaders so that other churches and pastors can learn how to do it.

Some pastors are afraid to follow our example. They fear that emphasizing prayer, calling people to deep commitment, and de-emphasizing large worship gatherings will cause their churches to collapse. But we must remember that our job is not to keep as many people as possible. Our job is to make sure that we're setting a biblical pattern. That's what the elders and I try to do. And isn't that why we got into ministry—because we read the Word of God and realized people aren't living holy lives and we wanted to help them? It was never a popularity contest, or I hope it wasn't. And yes, it could mean you lose a lot of people. It could mean that you don't even have enough people to sustain your salary. And that's a real test, but you keep doing it.

In the early days of our church I preached a particularly hard and convicting sermon. Afterward my worship pastor said to me, "Do you think anyone's going to come back next week?" And he was serious. And it was crazy but the next week's attendance was our biggest yet.

Of course, we have had people get upset and leave, and that's hard to take. But Jesus really didn't have a problem with turning people off if they weren't ready for the commitment. What I see in Scripture is that it's all or nothing. We are called to die to ourselves; it's complete death, surrender.

I tell people, "It's great that you're checking us out and learning, and I pray that you'll come to understand that God is good and nothing compares to him. I hope at that point you'll give your life to Jesus and follow him." The commitment to follow Jesus is like marriage. It's a lifelong commitment for better or for worse. And if someone is not ready to make that commitment, then they shouldn't get married.

On the other hand, when someone walks away because they're not ready for the commitment, we always have to check our own hearts and make sure we communicated with them in love. Early on when people first started to leave, we didn't show a lot of love or compassion. We sort of considered it a victory that people walked away. We had shown them the truth about their commitment. There was some arrogance in us, and that breaks my heart. Even now it's always hard when a person leaves. And so we rally around each other, encourage one another, and remind each other that this is going to happen, but we've got to keep teaching what we know to be true: the Christian life requires one's full commitment.

We are accused of being pharisaical for calling people to such a high commitment. We're often accused of becoming a cult because we call people to make that commitment. We define cults as communities overly committed to a belief system. By that definition Jesus would have been leading a cult. So today Mormons are willing to ride their bikes around town, Jehovah's Witnesses will knock on doors, but as Christians we don't have to do anything. We've been taught a watered-down version of following Jesus for so long that people think it's Christianity, but it's not biblical.

I have to be honest and say there were so many times I wanted to quit, because it is really painful when friends leave and your loudest fans become your loudest critics. It does get lonely. And it's hard when leaders who are with you start getting attacked. I get very defensive of my leaders because I love these guys. I don't want people to think it's easy to lead the church into greater depth and commitment. It stinks at times. But when you look back to the Word, you realize this is the way it's got to be, and you have peace.

6

SHARPEN YOUR SIXTH SENSE

———— ◉ ————

Practical Guidance for Making Good Decisions

BILL HYBELS

Several years ago a low budget movie became a box-office smash. The story line followed a boy who had a mysterious capacity to see what other people could not see—in this case seeing and interacting with people who weren't alive. The famous line in this movie, *The Sixth Sense*, was the boy's revelation, "I see dead people." It's eerie but quite memorable.

A pastor said to me, "Big deal. I see that at every deacon's meeting."

Many Christians, laypersons, and leaders alike, have a special intuition—a sixth sense, if you will. We probably all know people whose internal compass consistently works better than anyone else's in the room. Everyone else is trying to find the right direction in a particular circumstance, and then this individual, who's been quietly listening, speaks up and suggests a certain course, and everybody says, "That's it. Of course, that's it." How did he or she do that?

I know people who can perceive the future better than the average person. They can see the implications of current decisions on future realities. It's quite uncanny. Others can spot the one glittering diamond of opportunity where some see only a coal mine full of problems. I know leaders who can discern potential in an individual the rest of us would write off.

How do you explain those mysterious capacities?

Recently I've been thinking about the decision-making process. What contributes to this intuition? Can it be developed?

For thirty days I tried an experiment. I kept a pad of paper with me, and every time I made a decision, large or small, I jotted the decision down. After thirty days I reflected on those decisions to see if I could discern what factors informed my decision making. I wanted to understand this sixth sense, this mystery of my own intuition.

My conclusion? After considerable reflection, I believe that diligent, spiritually gifted, Romans 12:8 leaders and other Christians will, over time, construct a value system and experience base that informs each subsequent decision. This process enables Spirit-led men and women to get wiser and better as the years go by.

As I looked at my decisions, four distinct influences became apparent. These four sources inform most people's decisions, whether or not they're aware of them.

WHAT I REALLY BELIEVE

One decision that landed on my desk during that time involved one of our Willow Creek Association international offices. A senior leader, who subsequently left our employ, had made multiple questionable financial commitments. There were no signed contracts or paperwork to reference, but people were asking us to pay them for work they had done.

When asked what we should do, I answered instantaneously and intuitively: "Pay them. All of them. Pay whatever they ask."

As a Dutchman, parting with any amount of money is emotionally wrenching for me. But this decision was easy. I didn't have to hire a consultant or consciously pray about it. It wasn't even really economic in nature. The decision virtually made itself because of three bedrock foundations of my life.

1. *If I honor God in everything, God will honor me.* This is not a wall-plaqued nicety. This is a bedrock, unshakable-to-the-core-of-my-being belief. I really believe that the sovereign God will show his divine favor to anyone who consistently attempts to honor God in absolutely everything.

Conversely, if I dishonor God in any way, if I take shortcuts in life or in ministry, if I compromise my character, if I fail to keep my word, if I fail to obey promptings that he calls me to obey, I really believe that help from heaven is no longer guaranteed. God might give it in his grace, but I can't expect it. And I'm not a good enough leader to lead without help from heaven.

2. *People matter.* God has only one true treasure in this cosmos, and it's people. Therefore, I really believe that if I treat as valuable what God treasures most in this world, He will empower my efforts.

So whenever there's a "people component" to a decision, my antenna goes way up. I often tell our board members: "Friends, if we're going to err on this one, let's err on the side of being gracious to people." When we stand before God someday, we may find we extended too much grace sometimes, but we sure don't want to find out we erred on the other side.

In Luke 18 Jesus describes an unjust judge who had "no fear of God and no respect for people." He didn't worry about honoring God; he made whatever decisions would favor himself. And since he didn't care that people mattered, he had no respect for them. His decisions were informed by a faulty belief system that led to corruption. My resolve is to never resemble that judge.

3. *The church is the hope of the world.* Most people mistakenly

assume that I'm pretty intense about everything in life. Not true. Ask my close friends. I don't get amped up about restaurants, clothes, cars, recreation, money, politics, or most things in life. But without apology I get charged about this thing Jesus calls his bride, the church. Accuse me of being intense about the church, and I stand guilty as charged.

I'm all over any decision that has major implications for the future, health, unity, or effectiveness of the church—I'm all over that. I'll do almost anything or pay almost any price to make sure the church is well led. What do you really believe? Identifying your core beliefs will sharpen your effectiveness.

WHAT WOULD A BETTER LEADER DO?

My decisions are often informed by what I know others would do in a similar situation—people who are wiser, more gifted, more experienced than I am. Some of these people I know personally. Some I've never met, but they've mentored me by their books and tapes.

Different kinds of decisions prompt me to look to different kinds of leaders. Some decisions involve risk, and you have to consider a serious downside. The person who speaks to me most when I'm doing risk assessment is my dad. He has been dead for almost twenty-five years, but he still powerfully affects my risk management through what I observed in him.

Some people are extravagant risk takers who bet the farm again and again. And what happens when you bet the farm again and again? Eventually you lose the farm. On the other hand, some leaders are risk averse. They never take a risk.

My father was a calculated risk taker. He provided steady, consistent oversight for his core businesses. But he used to tell me, "Billy, if you don't take a flyer once in a while, you'll never learn anything, and life will get very boring." I think the expression "take a flyer" came from pilots testing new airplanes. My dad took his share of flyers in business—new ideas, new strategies, new products. He took some risks with people. Some flew really well; others crashed and lost a lot of money. But after a crash he would tell me the lessons he had learned during the adventure. And he would say, "It's not the end of the world. And it was sure fun to try."

My dad was almost impervious to the naysayers around him. When told his new idea was crazy, he would smile broadly and securely and say, "You're probably right. We'll all know in a few months, won't we?"

He wasn't a careless, always-bet-the-farm risk taker, nor was he risk averse. He just felt that a calculated flyer here and there would keep him learning and growing.

That approach continues to inform my decision making. We're taking a flyer right now with Willow Creek's regional ministry centers. We don't know if they're going to work. It's a calculated risk. But what often gives me the guts to pull the trigger is the influence of my dad.

Some leaders bet the farm too often and kill their churches. They must have someone in their heads they really respect—maybe a commodities trader—who thrives on risk. Others haven't taken a flyer in a decade, probably influenced by a respected voice that says, "Risk is bad. Failure is worse than never trying."

Who is informing your attitude toward risk? Is it the right person?

Many other kinds of decisions come to me.

How to handle underperforming staff? I look to two leaders— Jesus and Peter Drucker—and in that order. Jesus said, "the labourer is worthy of his hire."[23] The implication is that an employer owes a productive worker appropriate wages.

Conversely, if a worker is not performing worthy service, their wages should cease or decrease. Peter Drucker told me once, "Bill, when it comes to paid staff, even church staff, non-performance is unacceptable." I've never forgotten that.

So when we have an underperforming staff member, we call it what it is: unacceptable. Then we try to discern the cause. Is it poor job fit? Lack of training? Unrealistic expectations? We can address those. Or is it poor work habits? A bad attitude? A character flaw? An inability to work well with others? From time to time we've had to invite people off our staff. We do it lovingly. We often offer support and severance. But what Jesus and Peter Drucker said keep echoing in my mind.

Other decisions deal with issues of excellence. I think of two businessmen: Ed Prince and Rich DeVoss. They set excellence levels in their businesses and personal lives that seemed, as I began to really know them, so appropriate. Some people are too perfectionistic; others have an "anything will do" attitude. Ed and Rich model the right balance for me.

Another issue that lands on my desk is bureaucracy. One of our leading lay leaders will contact me totally frustrated and say, "What does a person have to do around here to get a simple yes or no? It's been three, count them, three months since I asked permission to do this. I don't even care what the decision is anymore or how you make it. Flip a coin, or call the Psychic Hotline. Just make a decision."

This is happening more and more at Willow Creek, and it's driving me nuts. But two business leaders that I've never met are helping me. I've read most of what they've written and much that's been written about them—Jack Welch from General Electric and Lou Gerstner from IBM. When Lou Gerstner took over IBM, he said that getting a decision made around there was like trying to swim upstream in a river of peanut butter. So he declared war on indecision, and for the most part he's winning the war. Jack Welch identified as his number two value at GE the ruthless eradication of bureaucracy.

When I receive an S.O.S. from anyone at church who says, "Will someone make a decision?" Lou Gerstner and Jack Welch come to mind, and they motivate me to take action fast.

So I'll have my assistant call all the affected parties to my office, and I'll say, "We're not leaving this room until we have an answer to the question that's been waiting for twelve weeks. So roll up your sleeves. We're making a decision."

I'm not advocating short circuiting due process. But timely decision making is essential for the life of a growing church. People deserve timely decisions. It wrecks morale to live in a constant stream of peanut butter.

There are many other types of decisions. For theological decisions I've had Dr. Bilezikian in my head for thirty years. With relational and psychological decisions I have two counselors who help me. In ethical and moral decisions my hero is the Old Testament leader Joseph, one of the few major leaders of all time of whom it was said he had a thoroughly clean record.

It's important to read, to be around others, to be exposed to people and principles that will inform your daily decisions and influence your intuition.

PAIN

The third major data source that impacts my decision making is pain from prior decisions that went bad. Sometimes someone will be trying to persuade me to go along with their concept, and in midsentence—almost as if they're stepping on a landmine—I break in and say, "That's not going to happen."

When they ask why, I'll say, "We tried that very thing fifteen years ago. We thought we were smart and we got whacked. Then we tried it again ten years ago. We got whacked again. We thought we were smarter three years ago, and we really got whacked. We have exceeded our whack quotient. Sorry. Your proposal is DOA, dead on arrival. Let it go."

One of the advantages of experience is that you've filled a pain file with enough jagged-edged memories that your intuition is poised and ready to wave the "go slow" flag when the likelihood of more pain appears on the horizon. Younger, less-experienced people are still busy collecting their whacks, and that's just life. Isn't it?

Pain is a fantastic teacher. When I do mentoring sessions with pastors, after dinner sometimes we'll put our feet up and tell each other the lessons we've learned the hard way, stuff we'll never do again. And I've heard some doozies.

- "I'll never make my mother-in-law the head elder again."
- "I'll never give a new youth pastor the church credit card for a weekend retreat."
- "I'll never let a guest speaker preach on signs and wonders while I'm on vacation."
- "I'll never tell the worship dancer, 'Just wear whatever you want when you dance.'"

Pain is a very effective teacher. And it's wise to learn from the pain of others.

PROMPTINGS BY THE HOLY SPIRIT

A year ago I was being pressured by our programming team to decide on the topic for our January weekend series. As I wrestled with my decision, the Holy Spirit nudged me as definitely as I've ever received a prompting: "Preach on love."

I argued back: "You've got to be kidding. That's too mushy for January. People need their annual January body slam like 'Fly Straight This Year,' 'Lose Weight,' 'Slow Down,' 'Get Out of Debt,' 'Stop Sinning,' 'Grow in God.' You know, January stuff!"

But after a few days, the Holy Spirit just wore me down: "Will you trust me on this one?"

So I did a series called "Graduate-Level Loving." And it received one of the highest responses of any series in recent years. And it was prompted more by God than my pastoral common sense. The decision to start Willow Creek in the first place wasn't a carefully calculated business plan. It was just a prompting. The same with the decision to focus on seekers, to utilize the arts, and to do our believer service midweek.

All this defied conventional wisdom. It was simply Spirit prompted.

So many of our best staff and volunteers wound up in the positions they're in not because we brilliantly placed them but because the Holy Spirit prompted them.

That thirty-day decision-making evaluation was a valuable exercise for me because it reminded me again what Scripture teaches: "those who are led by the Spirit of God are the children of God."[24]

Yes, we must use wisdom and good judgment as we lead our churches. But just as surely we must keep an ear tuned to heaven at all times, listening for the quiet whisper of the Holy Spirit, who from time to time speaks into our decision making.

I used to think all strong Christians did this regularly. But I don't take that for granted anymore. Do you really have an ear tuned to heaven? Is there enough quietness integrated into your life so you can hear the Spirit when he whispers? Do you obey the Spirit when he informs your decision making?

The Holy Spirit is a supernatural data source all his own, a source that supersedes all the other data sources and sharpens your sixth sense.

7

READING THE BIBLE SPIRITUALLY

———————— ◉ ————————

Ancient Practices Help Us Listen to the Bible,
Not Just Study It

EUGENE PETERSON

The Bible is not a textbook. Nor is it a manual to be studied, mastered, and mechanically applied. Instead, I believe we should listen to the Word of God and reflect upon it like poetry till it infiltrates the soul. I have found that the ancient practice of *lectio divina* is a way to listen humbly to Scripture and experience transformation. Let's explore how spiritual reading of the Bible allows us to slow down and listen once again to God.

What is *lectio divina*? Here is Richard J. Foster's excellent explanation:

> [L]ectio is a way of allowing the mind to "descend" into the heart, so that both mind and heart might be drawn into the love and goodness of God. Our goal is immersion. . . .
>
> In its classic form, lectio comprises four elements, although there are many variations on them with different wording and emphasis: *lectio* (reading with a listening spirit), *meditatio* (reflecting on what we are "hearing"),

oratio (praying in response to this hearing), and *contemplatio* (contemplating what we will carry forward into our lives). [We can also] refer to these basic elements of lectio as *listening, reflecting, praying,* and *obeying.* When these elements are combined—regardless of sequence, for they overlap and intermingle in a circular rather than a linear way—they lead the human spirit into a dynamic interaction with the Holy Spirit.[25]

I cannot remember when I started practicing *lectio divina*, but I was doing it intuitively long before I ever heard the term. In high school I was very much involved in poetry. You cannot read a poem quickly. There's too much going on there with its rhythms, alliterations, and layers of meaning. You have to read poetry slowly to absorb it all. When I was a student, I began to realize that the psalms were poems, and I began reading them and praying them as I would read poetry.

With this foothold in the psalms, I began to read all Scripture in this way. The first time you read a poem, you usually don't understand it. You've got to read it ten times or more. You've got to listen to it. That's just like the four steps of *lectio divina*. The four steps are not sequential; they're more like a spiral staircase. You keep going around and around, coming back to this step and over to that one. It's fluid.

I felt that this way of reading the Bible was important, even critical, to an effective immersion in Scripture. Therefore, I naturally wanted it to spread throughout my congregation. Toward that end, we formed small groups. People called them "Bible study groups," but that turned out to be a problem. When you put the word "study" in the name of a biblical activity, people think the goal is to master information. So they think the Bible is something you try to under-stand and explain. That is a huge barrier to break through. In fact, I can't say that I was very successful at it.

We quit calling our clusters "Bible study groups." I renamed them "conversation groups." We had conversations with the Bible. We would take a passage and listen to it; different people read it in different voices and then we tried to hear the poetry of the language, the sounds, and the message. I took notes as people shared, and then after an hour I would finally bring out some commentaries. I would show them that through our conversations, we had uncovered virtu-ally everything the commentary offered. I was trying to break the stronghold that academic scholarship has over us. We don't trust ourselves to encounter God's Word.

I should make it clear that I am not opposed to Bible study aids such as—dictionaries, concordances, and commentaries. They all have their good uses, but they sure get in the way of listening to the text. There is nothing terribly difficult in the Bible—at least in a tech-nical way. It is written in street language, common language. Most of it was oral and spoken to illiterate people. They were the first ones to receive it. When we make everything academic, we lose something important.

So why don't we automatically or intuitively read the Bible more reflectively? It's due largely to the way we're educated. When you've spent twelve, fourteen, or eighteen years in school, your habits form in a non-reflective way. And this is not a bad thing; it isn't a school's job to make us reflective. We go to school to learn information. We need to pass examinations and be able to read and retain. But most of us have never been taught to read and listen reflectively.

This kind of reflective reading, *lectio divina*, is what we should be teaching our churches to do, but it's not something you just learn and teach as you do facts and data. Reading the Bible not for information but to hear its voice speak to you takes practice. Pastors have to practice it first; they must enter into it. And in order to do that, pastors simply have to quit being in such a big hurry. Pastors are the busiest people in the world—always making an appointment or rushing to a meeting. They have no time to listen, and therefore they cannot teach others to listen.

In fact, I think we pastors are the worst listeners. We're so used to speaking, teaching, and giving answers. We must learn to be quiet, to quit being so verbal, to learn to pay attention to what's going on, and to listen. This is not only about listening to the Bible, it's about listening to people—taking time to hear the nuances in their voices and language and enter into what we're hearing. We're all very poorly educated in this business.

I know that as our world becomes more technological with more ways to communicate, it becomes harder for pastors to slow down and listen. But who else is going to do it if not pastors? No one else has the opportunity and the calling we have. If you look at it strictly from a professional point of view, we are the only identifiable group in society commissioned to pray, reflect on Scripture, and listen. And we are part of a spiritual Christian culture based on the Word. Pastors have got to learn to take words more seriously—not just as information or doctrine or rules. If we don't, who will?

When I challenge pastors to slow down, listen, and reflect, they tell me they would lose their jobs if they lived that way. And they might be right. I was called to my church when it was a new congregation. I was the only pastor most of the people had ever known. They became accustomed to me and my perspective on ministry. After being there about ten years, I realized there probably wasn't another church in the country that would hire me. No one else would put up with my more reflective, less frenetic way of living and working.

I do know a significant number of pastors who have slowed down to really listen. But they made a deliberate choice to do it. I have one friend who just resigned from his eight-hundred-member church though he had no other call. His criterion for accepting another church is that it must be less than one hundred members. There are pastors choosing this kind of life, but you don't usually hear about them.

I don't want to mislead you into thinking that smaller churches are more conducive for pastors to foster listening lives. I think you can do it in any size congregation, but the pastor must want to do it. And he must be willing to set aside the time to do it.

If a pastor starts listening to Scripture reflectively, his preaching will become more conversational and probably less polished. In the last class I taught at Regent, an obviously irritated young woman came up to me and said, "Dr. Peterson, three times during your lecture you did not say anything for twenty seconds. I know because I timed you. I'm from Hong Kong. In Hong Kong, teachers go: Bang! Bang! Bang! Bang! I want my money's worth."

We're going to have people like that—people who want very polished and efficient teaching. But I try my best to discourage it. When I see people in my congregation taking notes during the sermon, I stop and say, "Put your pencils away. I want you to listen. Listen to the Word of God. It's not something for you to figure out; it's something for you to respond to." Inducing this kind of change in thinking is slow work, and pastors are not patient people. It's something we must learn, and the very discipline of *lectio divina* will help us.

But, you may ask, what about right doctrine? Isn't it possible that people will mishandle Scripture if they engage it through conversation and *lectio divina* reading rather than rigorous and analytical study? Of course there are going to be misunderstandings—that goes with language. How many times in a marriage do a husband and wife misunderstand each other? And those misunderstandings don't occur because they used incorrect grammar.

But if we are part of a community where the Scriptures are honored, I don't think we have to worry too much. The Spirit works through community. Somebody will have a stupid, screwy idea. That's okay. We pastors must remember that we are not theology policemen. The point of having creeds and confessions and traditions is to keep us in touch with the obvious errors. Because we have those resources, I don't think we have to be anxious about it. If readers open their hearts to Scripture, God will speak to them.

8

TAME THE RESTLESS EVIL

———— ◉ ————

The Habit of Speaking Carefully

STEVE MAY

My friend Joi told me that when she was growing up, her parents invented a ploy to keep her from talking all of the time. They told her that people are allowed only so many words in one lifetime, and when they use up those words, they die. So, Joi developed a habit of using words sparingly. She told me she would often go an entire day without speaking a word, and at the end of the day she would think to herself, "I just added one whole extra day to my life!"

Joi seems to have survived her parent's trick with little damage; she's certainly never at a loss for words today. Nevertheless, I wouldn't recommend that parents use this strategy on their children. However, there is no question that it is good idea for us to teach our children—and to practice for ourselves—the art of speaking carefully.

The book of Proverbs has much to say about how we manage our words. Your ability or inability to control your tongue will determine more than anything else the level of success you enjoy in your relationships. If you can't seem to say the right thing, and you constantly seem to say the wrong thing, you may find yourself someday all alone, alienated from everyone in your life.

Some people find it easy to express themselves and have no trouble saying what is on their minds. We usually refer to these people as brilliant conversationalists. Some of them can talk on and on and on, use countless words, and never get around to saying anything at all. But we all know there is more to speaking effectively than being able to string words together.

I was watching the old *Dick Van Dyke Show* recently, and he was at a party filled with pseudo intellectuals. Dick got trapped into a one-sided conversation with a self-absorbed philosophy professor. One of the other guests said, "Isn't Dr. So and So brilliant?" Dick Van Dyke replied, "He has the ability to say things which are on the surface seemingly vague, but in reality are actually meaningless." That sums up the way many people make conversation.

The Bible teaches a different approach to conversation. It teaches us to use our words sparingly and to speak with caution.

I read the other day that the Ten Commandments contain 297 words. Psalm 23 has 118 words, and the Lord's Prayer is 56 words long. Yet, in a recent report, the Department of Agriculture needed 15,629 words to discuss the pricing of cabbage.

It's not using a lot of words that makes a difference; it's using the right words.

We need to get into the habit of speaking carefully. We need to learn to think first, talk second. Before you speak, here are some things to consider.

WE SHOULD FIRST CONSIDER NOT SAYING ANYTHING AT ALL

I'm going to tell you three things that, if you will take them to heart, will absolutely liberate you and revolutionize every relationship you have. The first is to learn that we don't have to yield to the impulse to open our mouths at all. Let's consider four benefits of keeping quiet when you're bursting to speak.

1. *We don't have to say everything we know.* I was having dinner with friends one evening and we began discussing Christian music. One lady named an artist and said, "He's my absolute favorite. I am so blessed when I listen to his music." Another person at the table said, "Oh really? Well, a person in my church was in a twelve-step group for overeaters and that singer was also in the group. Did you know that he's bulimic? He's been gorging and purging since he was a teenager." Now, he didn't have to tell us that. For starters, I would prefer not to hear about gorging and purging while I'm trying to eat. But more importantly, there's a reason why those groups all have the name "anonymous" in the title; people's privacy should be respected.

Blabbing that little bit of inside information did not build up the group, edify anyone, or bring glory to Christ. Just because we know something about someone doesn't mean we have to spill it. Now, if at some time in the future this particular Christian artist decides to publicly discuss his struggle with food addiction, that's his choice. Until then, it's his personal business.

You may know something about someone, but just because you know it, and just because it's true, doesn't mean you have to say it. If what you say does not build up others and bring glory to the name of Christ, then you're better off keeping your mouth shut.

Solomon put it this way: "A man of knowledge uses words with restraint."[26] Before we speak, let's consider saying nothing at all because we don't have to say everything we know.

2. *We don't have to say everything we think.* Some people believe they know a little bit more about every subject than anyone else, and they believe it is their duty to wax eloquent whenever the chance presents itself. Whatever subject comes up in conversation, whether

it's the stock market, computers, criminal justice, football, politics, or religion, they believe they have the first and final word on the matter. And, of course, they share it with you.

We can fall into this habit unintentionally, but we need to watch out for it. Several years ago my sister said to her only brother, "For once I would like to bring up a topic in conversation without having to listen to you pontificate about it for fifteen minutes." My sister's only brother has since tried his best to follow her suggestion.

Do you remember the character on *Cheers* named Cliff Clavin? He was constantly saying out loud everything he was thinking. No matter what subject came up in conversation, he had something to say about it. He was a self-proclaimed authority on anything and everything. Because of this, he was also the object of a lot of jokes. I heard someone say that in just about every group of friends there is someone like Cliff Clavin. If you look at your group of friends and don't see someone like him, maybe you should take a long hard look at yourself. You may be that person. We don't have to say everything we think. Before we speak, let's keep this principle in mind: Silence looks like knowledge. So, remember to think first and speak second.

3. *We can give the impression that we are wise if we keep silent.* Solomon tells us that, "Even a fool is thought wise if he keeps silent."[27] I took this verse into consideration a few years ago when I started a new job with a software publishing company. We were developing a new product in a joint venture with IBM, and my first week on the job was spent in all-day planning sessions at IBM's Lexington, Kentucky, plant. At that time my computer knowledge was extremely limited. I could spell "IBM"—that was all I knew about computers. As we sat through these eight-hour sessions day after day, terms that I didn't understand kept flying through the air, such as "config-dot-

sys," "OCR readability," "file buffering," and on and on. Throughout the meetings I kept nodding my head and saying things like, "I can't argue with that." Then, when we began to discuss parts of the project that I actually knew something about, I was able to make a significant contribution. My comments carried more weight because I hadn't blown my credibility by trying to talk about something I knew nothing about.

4. *We don't have to repeat everything we hear.* The problem with repeating gossip is that there is a better than even chance that what we heard isn't completely true. Gossip tends to get embellished as it is passed from person to person.

Gossip is a subject that we do not take seriously enough. We say things like, "I'm going to go visit so-and-so and catch up on the latest gossip." We say it like there's nothing wrong with doing that. To a certain extent, 'catching up on gossip' is just a figure of speech, but it's too often an all too accurate description of the way we make conversation. Do you know what Solomon says about gossips? "A perverse man stirs up dissension, and a gossip separates close friends."[28] That's something new to think about. Does it ever occur to us that when we say bad things about someone, God considers our actions perverted? It may seem hard to believe, but that is what the Bible says. In my humble opinion, the truer it is, the juicier it is, the more despicable it is to God when we repeat it. God would much rather we keep quiet about it.

Another of Solomon's proverbs tells us that "He who covers over an offense promotes love, but whoever repeats the matter separates close friends."[29] Repeating everything we hear destroys friendships. This is why we need to think before we speak and consider whether we should say anything at all. We don't have to repeat everything we hear.

WE SHOULD CONSIDER WHETHER WE
HAVE ALL THE FACTS

The first step to managing our mouth is to consider not saying anything at all. The second step is discerning whether or not we have all the facts.

Richard Jewell was the security officer who was first on the scene when the bomb exploded at the 1996 Olympics in Atlanta. He acted conscientiously and courageously, and he was, indeed, quite a hero. Then, as is typical in such events, the FBI developed suspicions about Jewell and began to consider him a suspect in the bombing.

The FBI was just doing its job by suspecting everyone. However, the media went wild with the story. *The Atlanta Journal-Constitution* printed a story packed with innuendos and misleading comments. *The New York Post* called him a "fat, former failed sheriff's deputy" in a story that crossed the line between reporting him as a possible suspect and declaring him guilty. Even former newscaster Tom Brokaw compromised his credibility by saying, "They probably have enough to arrest him right now, probably enough to prosecute him. But you always want enough to convict him."

As it turned out, Richard Jewell didn't plant the bomb. He really was a hero. He put his life in danger to save other people and he was ripped to shreds by the press. For once, the media was held accountable. A number of news organizations, including NBC, settled with Jewell for an undisclosed amount rather than go through the humiliation of a public trial.

This event taught us a couple of things. For instance, just because Tom Brokaw says something, it doesn't mean it's true. We need to remember when we watch the news, there is a very real possibility we're getting only a fraction of the story.

Another thing it taught us was that we can do a lot of damage by speaking before we get the facts, and some of the damage caused by speculating and speaking will come back our way. We may never find ourselves in the kind of jam NBC was in after reporting lies about Richard Jewel, but we can be sure that if we open our mouths before we get the facts, we are courting disaster for ourselves and everyone else involved. As Solomon says, "He who answers before listening— that is his folly and his shame."[30]

I remember a few years ago watching my boss fly off the handle because he thought he had been overbilled by a supply company. He screamed at the employee that should have caught the "mistake," then he called the supply house and yelled at them for a while, and he cancelled his contract with them. A little while later, he found out that he was wrong. He tried to apologize to the employee, but it was too late. She had already turned in her resignation. He called the supply house and asked to have his contract reinstated. They told him they would renew the contract, but at a higher rate. That fifteen minutes he spent jumping to the wrong conclusion ended up costing him dearly.

It reminds me of another of Solomon's proverbs: "A fool's talk brings a rod to his back, but the lips of the wise protect them."[31]

This is why we have to think first and speak second. Let's make sure we have all the facts. Remember Solomon's wisdom: "A man of knowledge uses words with restraint."[32] Before we open our mouths, we should consider carefully whether or not we have the facts.

WE SHOULD CONSIDER THE BEST WAY TO SAY WHAT NEEDS TO BE SAID

This is the third step in managing your mouth. We don't live in a Pollyanna world, and sometimes we have to say some things that aren't pleasant to say. But our words will carry more weight if we take the effort to say them well. As Proverbs says, "A man finds joy in giving an apt reply—and how good is a timely word!"[33] It takes effort—and a lot of thought—to make sure we say the right thing the right way.

A state trooper pulled a man and wife over for speeding on a deserted road. Since the road was clear and the weather was fine, the trooper told them he would let them off with a warning. He even complimented the man and his wife for wearing their seat belts. At that point the woman leaned over and said, "Well, officer, when you drive the speeds we do, you have to wear your seat belt." That's when the trooper decided to write the ticket after all.

That's an example of what can happen when we don't think before we speak. It's also an example of not considering the best way to say something.

There's an old story about a man who fixed his wife a sandwich. One of the pieces of bread he used was the heel. When he gave her the sandwich, she blew up and said, "I am so sick of you giving me the heel on every sandwich you make. You've been doing this for twenty years. Why do you insist on doing this to me every time?" The husband looked at her and said quietly, "Because the heel is my favorite piece."

Now, that guy knew the right thing to say. Apparently he understood what Solomon meant when he said, "A gentle answer turns away wrath, but a harsh word stirs up anger."[34]

If you need to confront your spouse, or your child, or an employee about a problem in your relationship, you should take the time to find the right way to go about saying it. You need to ask yourself, "How can I say this in such a way that it will build them up, and encourage them to do what is best for them?"

A woman once said to me, "My husband has a way of telling me to do something that makes me want to do the exact opposite of whatever he says." A caveman might say that this man's wife needs to learn how to submit. I would be more inclined to say that the husband needs to learn how to communicate with his wife in a gentler manner.

Let's look for the best way to say what needs to be said. We read in Proverbs, "The tongue has the power of life and death, and those who love it will eat its fruit."[35] When we speak to one another, we should keep these words in mind.

WE NEED TO ALWAYS THINK BEFORE
WE SPEAK

The Bible says so much about speaking carefully that I could write a book on this subject alone. Words have tremendous power, and we need to make sure we use them carefully. Solomon tells us, "He who guards his lips guards his life, but he who speaks rashly will come to ruin."[36]

It's not true that God only gives us a certain number of words to speak in our lifetime. It's not true that when our words are used up, our life comes to end, but it is true that there is great danger in talking too much, especially when we speak before we think. As Solomon puts it, "When words are many, sin is not absent, but he who holds his tongue is wise."[37]

We don't have to take a vow of silence, but all of us would benefit from making a commitment to think first and speak second. And while we're thinking, we can consider whether or not we should say anything at all. We can consider whether or not we have all the facts, and we can consider what the best way is to say what needs to be said. In guarding our lips this way, we guard our lives, we strengthen our relationships, and we build up others to a closer walk with Christ.

PART III

WASHOUTS AND DETOURS

Not long ago, the four-lane Interstate 5 freeway bridge on the Skagit River near Mount Vernon, Washington suddenly collapsed and fell fifty feet into the river.

An Associated Press account the next day reported that "Dan Sligh and his wife were in their pickup on Interstate 5 heading to a camping trip when a bridge before them disappeared in a 'big puff of dust.'

"'I hit the brakes and we went off,' Sligh told reporters from the hospital, adding he 'saw the water approaching . . . you hold on as tight as you can.'"[38]

There isn't a GPS unit or smartphone maps app in the world that could have helped Dan Sligh and his wife in that moment before the 1,112-foot steel-truss bridge suddenly plunged into the chilly waters below.

Things happen. Trouble flashes out of a calm, blue sky. And even supports in our life that we imagined to be sturdy and simply took for granted can collapse beneath our feet.

Nothing is sure in this journey of ours, except our God, our eventual destination, and the simple fact that we will have trouble along the way. Jesus said so himself: "*In this world you* will *have trouble. But take heart! I have overcome the world.*"[39]

In this section, Tullian Tchividjian, Gordon MacDonald, and Mark Buchanan encourage us with their experiences in dealing with unexpected troubles and unlooked-for hardships that delay our plans or send us off on a bumpy detour through an unfamiliar landscape.

9

TROUBLE HAPPENS

———————— ◉ ————————

What Suffering Will Do for You

TULLIAN TCHIVIDJIAN

Every time I preach through a book of the Bible, I emphasize at the beginning that if we don't understand the context of the entire book, we might lose track of where we're going once we look at various parts and details. It's important that we understand why God inspired the book of Job to be written. Let's look at Job 1:13–22:

> Now there was a day when [Job's] sons and daughters were eating and drinking wine in their oldest brother's house, and there came a messenger to Job and said, "The oxen were plowing and the donkeys feeding beside them, and the Sabeans fell upon them and took them and struck down the servants with the edge of the sword, and I alone have escaped to tell you." While he was yet speaking, there came another and said, "The fire of God fell from heaven and burned up the sheep and the servants and consumed them, and I alone have escaped to tell you." While he was yet speaking, there came another and said, "The Chaldeans formed three groups and made a raid on the camels and took them and struck down the servants with the edge of

the sword, and I alone have escaped to tell you." While he was yet speaking, there came another and said, "Your sons and daughters were eating and drinking wine in their oldest brother's house, and behold, a great wind came across the wilderness and struck the four corners of the house, and it fell upon the young people, and they are dead, and I alone have escaped to tell you."

Then Job arose, tore his robe and shaved his head and fell on the ground and worshiped. And he said, "Naked I came from my mother's womb, and naked shall I return. The LORD gave, and the LORD has taken away. Blessed be the name of the LORD."

In all this Job did not sin or charge God with wrong. (ESV)

This and the next chapter of Job give us a unique glimpse of something that happened behind the curtain, in the heavenly realm. They tell us about a mysterious conversation between God and the devil. Job, the subject of the conversation, has absolutely no clue of what has taken place backstage. He just responds on the stage.

WE ARE ALL LIKE JOB

By looking at Job's response, we can feel the weight of his calamity. We all suffer like Job. We may not suffer precisely as he did, but we suffer in similar ways.

For instance, Job did not know why tragedy struck as capriciously and suddenly as it did. It just happened. There was no forewarning. One minute he was enjoying all of the blessings that God had granted him, and the next minute all of it was taken away in one clean swoop.

Tragedy came on him like a thief in the night, and that's the way it comes on us. There is usually no forewarning or explanation. We never know what's around the corner.

We can learn a lot from the way Job responds in his suffering. We are just like Job. We don't know what is going to happen in our lives. It's important to understand that, because it's one thing for Job to respond the way that he did had he been given forewarning and explanation, and it's another thing for him to respond that way when he had been given none.

SUFFERING EXPOSES WHO YOU REALLY ARE

My dad used to say that character is demonstrated more by our reactions than our actions. He was a psychologist. He understood how people functioned. He understood that what we are made of—who we really are—comes out in times of pain and desperation. Allen Redpath, a pastor in Chicago, used to say, "The flavor of a tea bag comes out best when you put it in hot water."

Job was put in some serious hot water. You can pretend to be someone you're not. You can manipulate people to believe something about you that's not true. You might succeed in doing this for a long time. But when suffering hits, when pain strikes, and when tragedy comes, who you really are inevitably comes out. Whatever masks you've been wearing go away. Whatever pretense you've been manufacturing goes away. God does us a remarkable favor by showing us how Job responds to a sudden strike of suffering. We learn from Job that who we are is exposed by our reactions to suffering.

Job's response has two parts: First, it is emotionally realistic. Second, it reveals the depth of his theological perspective. Job blessed God when he was hit with suffering. He said, "The LORD gave and the LORD has taken away. Blessed be the name of the LORD."[40] We also see the depth of Job's theological perspective at the end of the book when he says, "My ears had heard of you but now my eyes have seen you."[41] Through suffering, Job came to see, know, and trust God in ways that he did not before.

Chapter 1:1–5 sets the stage for the entire story of Job. As remarkable as he was in the beginning of the story, he still needed to be saved, rescued, redeemed, and changed. He still had growing to do. The same is true for you and me. It's what I call the salvation of the saved. Those who have been saved need to be rescued by God on a daily basis. Job 1:5 tells us that Job was a remarkably godly man, but he still had much to learn. God took him through a trying season in order to make him bigger, better, and brighter than he was previously. Job didn't know that in the beginning. He couldn't see the light at the end of the tunnel. He was hit by a freight train, and everything faded to black. Many of you know exactly how that feels.

GOD EXPECTS A REAL RESPONSE TO REAL PAIN

Let's look at Job's response: "Then Job arose and tore his robe and shaved his head."[42] Job didn't get the initial stage of bad news in August, the second stage in September, the third in October, and the fourth in November. He received it all on the same day. As one reporter finished explaining one disaster, another reporter began. Not only that, the reports became increasingly worse, culminating with the death of his ten children. All ten died on the same day, without warning or expectation. Job's response was realistic. He tore his robe, shaved his head, and fell on the ground, gasping for air, with his heart pounding. He felt absolutely paralyzed.

Recently, I read a book by preacher and theologian David Jackson titled *Crying out for Vindication: The Gospel According to Job*. The book begins like this:

I discovered Job when I was sitting by my wife's hospital bed, waiting for her to wake up after a miscarriage. We had prayed for this child's safety and salvation since before the child was conceived. We had prayed all that night that the child would survive the present crisis. The answer was no. I sat there, looking out the window of the hospital at sunrise, and watched a bird fly across a cloudless sky as the sun rose, and I asked the Lord, "How come that wretched bird could soar through such a sunrise, and our child, made in your image, never see the light of day?"[43]

When pain and tragedy strike, God expects from us an emotionally realistic response. Suffering is inevitable and unavoidable. None of us can escape it. Pain can be intense at times, as in the cases of death, disease, depression, and divorce. But even in the absence of severe crisis, pain is constant. Most of us have become so used to the steady drip of suffering and pain in our lives that we don't even realize that it's constant. But the truth is, we are broken people living in a fallen world with other broken people. You and I, whether Christian or not, have never known a day in which suffering is altogether absent. Because of sin, every day you live, from the day you were born till the day you die, is not what it ought to be. My ongoing struggles with others, with God, and with circumstances are all a part of suffering. Suffering is far more than just sudden tragedy. Life in this broken world is suffering. Pain is constant because nothing is what it ought to be.

Job—in a series of quick and major blows—loses his wealth, his children, his reputation, and his health (we see this in chapter 2). When Job responds by tearing his robe, shaving his head, and falling on the ground, it's important to notice that his emotional outburst is not condemned. "In all this Job did not sin or charge God with wrong."[44] God doesn't look on Job's emotional outburst and say, "Come on, get hold of yourself. Toughen up. Be a man. Don't you know that I'm God, and all of this has been done for a good reason?"

God didn't say any of that. The Bible says, "In all this Job did not sin." Suffering is real and painful. It's not imaginary. According to the Bible, it's an everyday part of our experience as Christians. Nowhere does the Bible brush lightly over pain. God never sanctions a "suck it up and deal with it" posture towards pain. Pain is real, and you don't want to make the mistake that Job's friends made. They were remarkable counselors to Job until they attempted to explain the reason for his suffering. For the first seven days, they simply sat with Job in silence, weeping with him without trying to give an explanation for what had happened. They had no idea what went on behind the heavenly curtain. Then they began to speculate arrogantly.

We're not acting theologically mature if we are always trying to come up with an explanation. Nobody—except God, the devil, and the angels in the courts of heaven—knew why Job experienced what he did. His friends didn't know, his wife didn't know, his servants didn't know, and he didn't know. And as we will see over thirty chapters, Job and his friends spend many words trying to figure out why such calamities struck Job down. They came up with reasonable explanations for why he suffered, as if that would ease the pain.

I often talk to people who say, "If I could just know from God why I'm suffering, I would be able to endure it." They believe an explanation from God would ease their pain. But then their hope wouldn't truly be in God; it would be in the explanation. If you do not go to your grave in confusion, you will not go to your grave trusting. Explanations are a substitute for trust.

GRIEF IS AN ACT OF WORSHIP

After all these calamities had struck Job down, we read: "And [he] *worshiped*."[45] The location of the word worshiped in the context of this passage implies that Job's expression of grief was in itself an act of worship. Scripture doesn't say that he grieved, got over it, and then worshiped. Job's expression of grief, his coming apart at the seams, was itself an act of worship. How can that be? Grief is an emotional acknowledgement that things aren't the way they should be. Grief acknowledges that the way God originally intended things to be has been vandalized. Grief involves a distant memory of what the world was like prior to the disobedience of Adam and Eve—a world full of justice, grace, and mercy. Grief also involves a cry for what will one day be a universal reality: a world without pain, disease, or conflict.

You may not realize it, but that's what happens when you grieve. You acknowledge that suffering should not happen. We all have an ideal of how things should be, and that ideal comes from God, because you were made in his image. Whether you have a relationship with Jesus or not, there's still something inside of you that recognizes suffering is unnatural.

So Christian grief is an act of worship because it is a statement of faith that one day things won't be this way. Romans 8 tells us that all of creation groans for renewal, and that we are "eagerly waiting for the adoption, the redemption of our body."[46] Christian grief is a cry for the renewal of the creation ideal. We are under the curse, and we long for that day when Jesus will come back to make all things new.

Whether you realize it or not, that is the song that underlies your grieving—a song that cries out for Christ's return. God didn't originally create a world where children die and things are stolen and lost. Our sin and disobedience caused things in this world to unravel. The storyline of the Bible proceeds like this: part one, God created all things good; part two, our sin broke every good thing that God made; part three, redemption in Christ makes all things new.

One day Jesus will come again to fix everything that we broke. He will put this world back in order. I love the way C. S. Lewis pictures it in *The Lion, the Witch, and the Wardrobe*. Narnia was covered in snow because it was under the curse of the White Witch. It was always winter and never Christmas. When Aslan, the rightful ruler of Narnia, began to approach the dark, cursed land, the snow began to melt. The White Witch could no longer operate on her sleigh. It didn't work on the grass or among the flowers.

When Jesus, our King, comes back, he will put this broken world back together again. You don't need to be ashamed of your grief, because your grief is a cry for that day—the day when we will enjoy sinless hearts and minds with disease-free bodies. Everything that causes pain and discomfort will be forever put away.

At times, Christianity is charged with being equivalent to stoicism. Some people believe that Christians don't face the hardships of life. Unfortunately, many Christians are guilty of giving the world that impression because they believe we're supposed to be happy in Jesus all the time. But that means that when pain strikes, we are called to put on a smiley mask and say that God is good. Certainly, Job says that God is good, but he does it while weeping and wailing. You're not proving to be strong and manly by suppressing your grief. You won't be helpful to someone experiencing grief if you say, "But you're a Christian, smile. Don't you know God is good all the time?" Yes, God is good all the time, but suffering in this fallen world is not. That's why God ordains tears.

The cross of Jesus proves that when it comes to pain and suffering, God is no stoic. The Father ordained the tears of the Son in the Garden of Gethsemane. You cannot look at the cross and the seven cries of our Savior as he hung upon it and say that God did not ordain Jesus' pain. Jesus knew while he was on the cross that it was only a matter of time before the pain would be over—before the wrath of his Father had been absorbed. He knew that the resurrection was coming, yet he still expressed grief and pain as he cried out to his Father for help.

Christianity is not stoicism. In fact, when you investigate other world religions, you discover that they all have a way of minimizing the reality of pain. Christianity is the only world religion that worships a God who suffers. We face reality head on because in the person of Jesus Christ, God has given us all the resources to handle pain in a way that enables us to demonstrate God's worth before the watching world.

UNDERSTANDING GOD'S GRACE

Job's response is not only emotionally realistic, it's also theologically deep. The first part is expected: "Then Job arose, tore his robe, and shaved his head; and he fell to the ground."[47] Weeping out loud, sitting in dust and ashes, shaving one's head, and tearing one's robe was a normal expression of grief in the ancient Near East. In the Bible, people grieved by covering themselves in dust and ashes. It was an expression that they were made from dust and to dust they would return. We are creatures; we are fallible, finite, and without God we are fully undone. Whether you're a Christian or not, you respond that way in times of tragedy, pain, difficulty, and trial.

The second part of Job's response, however, is absolutely stunning: "Naked I came from my mother's womb, and naked shall I return there. The LORD gave, and the LORD has taken away; blessed be the name of the LORD."[48] You don't have to know God to respond to grief in the expected way, as Job's grief is first described. But you can respond like Job does in the second way only if you know God. No matter how strong you are, you do not have the resources to deal with a tidal wave of pain and keep your footing. Job could respond the way he did in verse 21 only because he knew God.

It's important to see both parts of Job's reaction because if we did not have part one, we would conclude that part two was simply an expression of shock. If we only had part two without part one, we would assume Job went insane when he said, "Naked I came from my mother's womb and naked shall I return. The LORD gave and the LORD has taken away; blessed be the name of the LORD." If we didn't know about the first part of Job's reaction, we would assume he didn't understand what actually happened. God carefully, generously, and graciously gives us Job's emotional outburst before his expression of worship and theological depth. The second part of Job's response is just as real as the first part. If we didn't have part one, we would look at part two, shrug our shoulders, and say, "He's in a state of shock. Once he realizes what happened, he won't respond that way anymore."

We can respond decently in times of trial if we're in shock. Most of us don't fully realize what has happened until some time has passed. This is especially true when loved ones pass away. I watched this with my wife, Kim, when her father died several years ago. She was so strong for the rest of her family for the first twelve days after his death. But after that, she fell apart. God ordained shock for her so that in that moment she could be strong. But then the time came for her to deal with the emotion of her dad's death. Most of us deal with pain, tragedy, trial, and tribulation long after the event. It usually takes an extended period of time to process what happened.

Job demonstrates that it's possible to maintain joy in a season of suffering. But we must realize that this is not the same as ignoring the pain. Job demonstrates that it's possible to absorb the pain and maintain joy. In his second Corinthian letter Paul says, "We are afflicted in every way." He doesn't say we are afflicted in some ways. He says, "We are afflicted in every way, but not crushed; perplexed, but not driven to despair; persecuted, but not forsaken; struck down, but not destroyed."[49] Then he says, "We do not lose heart. Though our outer nature is wasting away, our inner nature is being renewed every day. For this slight momentary affliction is preparing for us an eternal weight of glory beyond all comparison."[50] Then Paul goes on to say, "We look not to the things that are seen."[51] We can't look to our children, our wealth, our health, or our status in this world for our security, identity, and value. Our value, worth, and identity are found in the things that are unseen and eternal.

The Apostle Paul suffered probably more than most of us will ever suffer in our lives. He was in three shipwrecks. He was able to say, "To live is Christ, and to die is gain."[52]

It is vitally important for us to realize that suffering itself does not rob you of joy; idolatry does. If you're angry, bitter, and joyless in the midst of your suffering, it means you've idolized whatever you've lost. Joylessness and bitterness in the crucible of suffering happens when we lose something we've held onto more tightly than God.

SUFFERING BRINGS FREEDOM

I want every Christian to experience Job's freedom—his rescue from bitterness and anger in the midst of suffering. Therefore, let me ask you a few diagnostic questions. How does your present disappointment, discouragement, or grief reflect what has actually captured your heart? When we depend on anything smaller than God to provide us with the security, significance, meaning, and value we long for, God will demonstrate his love for us by taking those things away. He will take them away, not because he's angry, but because he loves us and wants us to enjoy the freedom and security that comes from knowing Jesus.

Instead of looking to Jesus for our significance and value, we often look to insignificant things. When that happens, we become slaves. God comes after us in the person of Jesus Christ, not angrily to strip away our freedom, but affectionately to strip away our slavery to self so that we might become truly free. That's good news. The reason for our anger and bitterness in the crucible of suffering is that God is prying open our hands to take away something we've held onto more tightly than we've held onto him.

How did Job survive all this calamity? He survived because he had a robust theology of grace. If you don't know what grace is, you won't understand Job. Job knew that he was not entitled to anything he had. God held the title to everything in his life. Job was simply a steward. In Job 1:1–5 we learn that he was a good dad: he prayed for his children. He was generous. He gave God credit, honor, and glory for who he was. Job's theology of grace enabled him to say, "Naked I came from my mother's womb, and naked shall I return. The LORD gave, and the LORD has taken away." If he believed that he owned his children, his cattle, and so forth, he would have lived his life with a sense of entitlement. He would have responded to his suffering thinking he deserved better. Grace is the opposite of entitlement. While Job loved his children, his health, and his wealth, he realized he was only a steward of those things. He did not locate his identity and value in his possessions.

If the foundation of your happiness is your vocation, your relationships, or your money, then suffering takes your source of joy away from you. But if your ultimate value in life is God, then suffering drives you closer to your source of joy—God. Suffering exposes the foundation of your life.

Seven years ago, after forty-one years of marriage, my parents divorced. It wasn't because of infidelity or abuse, physically or emotionally. My family and I still scratch our heads and wonder exactly what happened. Was it really a case of irreconcilable differences? I don't think that's possible for Christians because of the power of the gospel. It was an incredibly painful time for my siblings and me. We experienced a happy, healthy, loving home growing up. We had remarkable parents, and they provided the stability we needed as children. I don't know what it's like for a mom and dad to go through a divorce while their children are young. All I know is that it's weird to watch your parents divorce in the stage of life where you have to explain it to your own kids.

The Bible states clearly that God hates divorce. It grieves his heart. There was nothing about my parents' divorce that seemed redemptive. I couldn't understand why God allowed it to happen. I was struggling with the whole situation, not simply because I was sad that my mom and dad apparently could not keep the promises they made to one another forty-one years earlier, but because part of my identity was wrapped up in being the son of my parents. I felt important because of their standing in society. My mom and dad were remarkable citizens and church people. Their reputation made me feel significant. I realized years later that much of the devastation I had experienced was due to the fact that I had idolized my parents and their reputation.

When you understand God's grace—that everything you need is in Christ—then pain leads to freedom. When you understand God's grace, you realize that deep suffering, as bad as it is, leads to deep surrender. Your pain can lead either to slavery or freedom. It doesn't matter if someone wronged you or if you wronged yourself. At this point, the circumstances of your pain become irrelevant. Suffering exposes what you're made of, and what you cling to becomes relevant. In the crucible of suffering, you can either become bitter or better. You can either become a slave to yourself, with a sense of entitlement, or you can be liberated by a biblical understanding of grace.

This means that sometimes God is actually saving us when it feels like he's killing us. This is displayed most perfectly in the cross. This is a broken world. It's messed up, and you're messed up. Everybody around you is messed up. You need help—otherworldly help. In the person of Jesus Christ, God has provided that help. The death of Christ gives life to sinners like you and me. Do you know him? Our desire is for all people to know Jesus, and we want them to know him in such a way that they can respond like Job did in the crucible of suffering: "Naked I came from my mother's womb, and naked shall I return. The LORD gave, and the LORD has taken away; blessed be the name of the LORD."

10

THE ART OF MANAGING CONFLICT

———— ◉ ————

When Conflict Occurs Where You Least Expect It

GORDON MACDONALD

One of our family scrapbooks contains a note written many years ago by our daughter's best friend, Cindy. It was written when the girls were both eight years old and inseparable. They walked to school together every morning, enjoyed frequent sleepovers, and consulted one another on homework assignments each night.

Then one day a tiny incident stressed their friendship. Our daughter, becoming impatient when Cindy would not walk fast enough on the way to school, called her a slowpoke.

It was impulsive, a bad choice of words. One can only guess what it may have meant to Cindy. At any rate there was instant enmity between the girls. That evening there was no collaboration on homework. An upcoming sleepover was canceled. And the following morning the girls walked to school by different routes.

A day later a note, the one in our scrapbook, came in the mail. Addressed to our daughter, it read: "You called me a slowpoke, and I am angry at you. Your [*sic*] no longer friend, Cindy." Could Cindy have been more specific? The issue, her feelings, the altered status of the relationship—all clearly defined in two sentences.

The separation lasted, at most, one more day. When both girls realized how much they missed each other, they offered mutual "sorrys" (one for walking too slow, the other for using the epithet "slowpoke") and resumed their friendship. Soon, it was as if nothing had come between them.

Yet something had happened; something had been learned. One girl had become aware of the importance of guarding her tongue lest an errant word hurt another's feelings. And the other learned not to overreact in a heated moment. Valuable lessons. If remembered, the "learnings" might save both of them in many of the inevitable quarrels they would experience in the future.

I recall wishing at the time that it would be nice if some of the adults in our church could deal with their prickly issues as clearly, as quickly, and as completely as the two girls had done. And what I wished for my congregation, I also wished for myself. In the field of human conflict, I was far from a genius.

A CONFLICT AVOIDER

I hated conflict as a child. When it occurred between my parents, I often felt a sense of responsibility to try and reconcile them. But I never succeeded because I was incapable of understanding the complexity of the underlying problems that so frequently separated them. When there was conflict between my parents and myself, I felt fear, humiliation, and a sense of insignificance because it never seemed (at least to me) that anyone cared to listen to my side of the story or to offer me the benefit of the doubt. No matter the issue, when adults were involved, I always seemed to come out the loser.

Thus, my preferred way of handling conflict in my younger years became the strategy of avoidance. How? By being super-nice and convivial, by taking care to say nothing that might offend or create controversy, by quickly backing down when opposed. If conflict was inescapable, I usually capitulated as soon as I could and opted for peace at any price. Additionally, I tried to stay away or to run from any relationship where I sensed the possibility of contentiousness.

I convinced myself that this was the Christian way, and that followers of Jesus should always seek peace and be loving. Thus it was, for the most part, that no one ever knew when I had strong feelings about this issue or that one. And no one knew, when they took advantage of my noncombative strategy, that I was inwardly hurt or angry, that I felt diminished. Unable to discern this, they simply assumed I was easy to get along with.

I envied people who seemed to say exactly what they thought with little concern for the results. I wished I could express my feelings and defend my opinions as strongly as they did. But unable to do this, I—best as I was able—kept most of my opinions and feelings to myself.

When I became an adult, I began to see that this policy of conflict avoidance could no longer be sustained if I desired a healthy marriage or if I aspired to some form of leadership. I was in danger of becoming permanently shallow and superficial, a person who seemed to stand for nothing of significance. This is the curse on someone who fears disagreement.

FACING INTO CONFLICT

Two experiences in particular forced me to face this deficiency in my life.

The first occurred when I met my wife-to-be, Gail. I was drawn to her because she was strong in spirit and mind. I enjoyed her company because she possessed points of view from which I could draw wisdom. I loved her because she affirmed my dreams and because she wanted to add to them. I desired to share life with her because we had complementary visions about how that life should be lived.

But here was my problem. You can't come close to a person of Gail's quality and develop connections such as I've just described if you want to avoid conflict all your life. Clashes of perspective and priority are simply part of the deal if you want to merge futures with a person of intellectual and spiritual vitality.

While I greatly desired what Gail might bring to our marriage, I came to see that some of it would come through criticism, through the clash of adverse opinions and judgments, through the realization that in more than a few cases, she might actually be smarter and wiser than I was. That meant that I would have to occasionally embrace her ways while surrendering mine.

A mutual friend, sensing that I was struggling with this matter, advised me just before our wedding, "God has given you a remarkable woman to marry. He means to teach you many things through her. Listen to her!" In order to make his point he repeated himself. "Listen to her! Even when she says things you find difficult to hear." This was new information to a man somewhat naïve in his understanding of conflict.

The kind of listening of which my friend spoke meant that I could no longer run away, no longer cover my ears and hide my eyes. Listening meant embracing the possibility that I might be wrong or misinformed. Listening meant discovering that others—like Gail, for example—often had better ideas than mine.

Of course, there was another side to this. Building a good marriage meant I also had to speak my mind and heart with respectful clarity. I had to assert my convictions and concerns. How does one do this if he's already chosen the agreeable anything-you-say approach?

The second incident involved a ministry colleague. An issue (not worth mentioning, not even well remembered) arose between us, and I felt more strongly about it than he did. Yet I could not bring myself to state my case and get the justice I felt I deserved. The moment called for sincere confrontation, but I could not make it happen. Those fears first generated in my childhood years blocked all attempts I wished to make to bring the issue to light and to deal with it.

The result? I became silent, sullen, withdrawn in our working relationship. Inside, I seethed and allowed a bitterness to take root in my soul. Soon I was under the influence of a hateful spirit.

A problem that could have been resolved in an hour of frank conversation became an interior, uncontrolled brush fire, and it affected me for months. Only when I became disgusted with myself did I find the power to both repent of my attitude and forgive what I thought was the offense of the other person.

I found this experience so distasteful that I vowed I would never again allow feelings of that sort to infest my spirit. And for these many years, I have been reasonably successful in keeping my vow.

My fledgling marriage taught me that conflict is unavoidable but there's an artful way to engage in it. My ministry experience taught me that conflict, left smoldering, will take on a life of its own, with destructive effect.

It was not easy to pull out the old wiring deep within me when it came to dealing with disagreeable situations. Whether it was my need to listen to the truth or my need to speak the truth to someone else, all the old tapes of my childhood played loudly in my mind. I had to reappraise my entire relationship to conflict. My ministry, maybe even my marriage, was on the line.

REDEEMING CONFLICT'S RAW MATERIALS

Little by little I learned what can happen (and what should happen) when conflict arises.

Conflict may be unavoidable, but there is an artful way to engage in it.

Searching the Scriptures for a better understanding of conflict, I was startled by the number of occasions where good (and not so good) people fell into situations similar to the one our daughter and her best friend had experienced.

Adam blamed Eve for his problems, thinking he could wiggle out of conflict. Abraham and Lot split their joint venture because of growing contentiousness among their servants. Brothers Jacob and Esau reached a point of resentment so great that one of them simply skipped town. Joseph had a legitimate case against his brothers but chose to end it in forgiveness. The Israelites constantly drained the spirit of Moses with their complaining. They may have left Egypt, but Egypt never left them.

There is Saul angrily chasing David through the wilderness, Ahab expressing antipathy toward the prophet Micaiah, Nehemiah fending off the efforts of saboteurs.

In the New Testament there is frequent squabbling among the disciples, the debates among the early Christians, and the messiness of life in the divisive church in Corinth. Each of these conflicts was different. Many ended badly (David and Absalom). Others ended with great grace, none better than the morning when Jesus made breakfast for the failed disciples and offered them another shot at being on the point of his mission to the world.

When I catalog the Bible's accounts of people at loggerheads, I gain courage in realizing that I am not alone in my struggle to do well when conflict arises.

I searched out mentors to learn how to be a man of greater candor. To know how to confront the associate who was under my organizational authority. To learn how to rebuke the person who needed firm pastoral influence. To master the ability to speak my heart to my young wife in a way that would not hurt her or tear at her self-confidence.

At the same time I wanted to appreciate the ways in which I could trim my emotions and my tendency to resist those who needed to be honest with me. If I was going to be the spiritual leader of a congregation, I would have to acquire a coolness of spirit so that I could engage in challenging conversation.

A breakfast with the chairman of our church board sharpened these intentions. I was a very young pastor, prone to making novice-level mistakes. The chairman often met with me to help me see these and evaluate different ways of doing things. On this particular day the conversation became difficult, and the chairman said some things I didn't want to hear. I revealed my feelings of hurt and frustration in a less than mature way. I'll never forget how he slapped his hand on the breakfast table to get my attention and said: "Pastor, you have a serious problem. You are too sensitive to criticism. You take too many things too personally. If you cannot hear the truth and deal with it, you'll not last long in your work. Get used to difficult conversations. You'll never be without them."

STEPS TO RESOLVING A CONFLICT

So I learned that the way of the leader, the way of a good friend, the way of one who wants to be a good husband or wife is the way of processing and managing conflict so that it reaps a positive benefit and is not destructive. I had to learn how to resolve conflict in much the same way our daughter and her friend Cindy learned to do it.

My own experiences have taught me that managing conflict is a five-step process. Let's look briefly at each step:

1. *Accept that conflict—the collision of two or more perspectives— is a necessary ingredient of any human relationship.* If we knew each other's hearts as well as did the first man or woman before the Fall ("the two were naked and unashamed"), we might reduce conflict. But, like an iceberg, there is too much of each of us beneath the perceptible level that is unknown and only comes out in the expressive moment. Blame it on sin, perhaps: we are always playing catch-up when it comes to understanding each other. Thus conflict comes.

2. *Recognize that each of us brings "baggage" from past experiences into present dealings.* Past fears or hurts or humiliations are likely to influence present circumstances. So when I feel irritable or angry at someone, I try searching my memory: are any issues from my past injecting themselves into my present?

3. *Remember that conflict need not be—and should not be—about winning or losing.* I have met more than a few people who need to win every dispute, dominate every conversation. I've often wondered if St. Paul wasn't a bit like that. Did he always have to be right?

4. *Decide to limit any kind of disagreement to the issue.* I find it tempting, if my position is weak, to attack the ways and means of the other person: question motives, complain about the way I feel treated, to rebalance the issue in my favor by bringing up other issues.

5. *Reach the terminal point in a conflict where adult versions of "sorrys" are said and solutions found.* Sometimes that means bending and compromising. Other times it means recognizing that another was "righter" and I was "wronger." And—after all of this—there are even times when I might be right but that it is appropriate, because of great love, to simply surrender my rights and to do it their way.

I discovered that healthy conflict should be about the energetic search for a better idea . . . or for personal insight . . . or for a more effective way of achieving something. It means that in critique or disagreement or misunderstanding, we give the other person the so-called charitable assumption that they too are seeking something that will mutually benefit us all.

The conflict over the allocation of funds for the relief of widows that threatened the early church is a remarkable case study in constructive conflict. One group of Christians (the Hellenists) contended that the Judean Christians were discriminating against them. Rather than trying to defend themselves, the Judeans were wise enough to consult and come up with a plan that was agreeable to everyone. The result? Leadership was redefined and reconfigured.[53] Everyone regained mutual respect for one another, and the church resumed growing.

Among the more difficult things I learned about conflict was the assumption that there was probably a kernel of truth in the opinions and positions of those who, while in conflict, might seem for the moment to be my worst enemy.

Through the years I came to realize that some of the most important insights I gained about myself came not from my friends but from my critics who, while playing rough, nevertheless alerted me to blind spots and inadequacies no one else had the courage to tell me about.

Yet, having said all this, there remains one more thing unsaid. Conflict carries within it an inherent danger: that the spiritual enemy (of whom the Bible says he seeks someone to devour[54]) loves to fan the flames of conflict so as to divide good people and shatter their ability to accomplish great things.

I have always felt saddened when I read in Acts 15 of the dissension that arose between Paul and Barnabas regarding second opportunities for young John Mark. Barnabas represented the case for a second chance; Paul, the case for disqualification. Unable to resolve these differences, the men parted company, and Barnabas disappeared from the pages of history. How could two men who had been so close in both friendship and apostolic passion permit their partnership to be dissolved? It is an urgent reminder to me that no relationship is exempt from destruction when conflict is improperly managed.

For many years my wife and I enjoyed a friendship with Dr. Paul and Edith Rees, who lived well into their nineties before going on to Jesus. Dr. Rees was best known for being a great pastor in Minneapolis for more than thirty years and for traveling the world on behalf of World Vision.

Sometime during their ninetieth year, the two of them spent a day with Gail and me. I asked Dr. Rees, "Do you and Edith ever fight? After all, you've been married more than sixty years."

"Oh, sure we do," Dr. Rees responded. "Yesterday morning was a case in point. Edith and I were in our car, and she was driving. She failed to stop at a stop sign, and it scared me half to death."

"So what did you do?" I asked.

"Well, I've loved Edith for all these years, and I have learned how to say hard things to her. But I must be careful because when Edith was a little girl, her father always spoke to her harshly. And today when she hears a manly voice speak in anger—even my voice—she is deeply, deeply hurt."

"But Paul," I said, "Edith is ninety years old. Are you telling me that she still remembers a harsh voice that many years ago?"

"She remembers that voice more than ever," Rees said.

"So how did you handle the situation yesterday?"

"Ah, I simply said, 'Edith, darling, after we've had our nap this afternoon, I want to discuss a thought I have for you. And when our nap was over, I did. I was calm; she was ready to listen, and we solved our little problem."

These are the words of a man who has learned that conflict is necessary, can be productive, but must be managed with wisdom and grace. By the time I reach ninety, I hope to be just like him. Why, by then, I may become as good at managing conflict as I once saw our daughter and her friend Cindy manage it.

11

BAD SITUATIONS ARE GREAT OPPORTUNITIES

———— ◉ ————

*Your Worst Nightmare May Cause
Someone Else's Sun to Rise*

MARK BUCHANAN

I had a Paul-like conversion.

There were no horses, voices, blindness—no bloody trail at my feet. But it was dramatic. Something like scales fell from my eyes. I stood in the shadow of Christ's cross and in the light of his resurrection. Christ met me, embraced me, forgave me, and gave me himself. I never looked back.

That was more than twenty-five years ago. For eighteen of those years I've been a pastor, a fact that has not yet ceased to amaze me: that God would take me, the worst of sinners, the least of the "apostles," and make me his chosen vessel to carry his name before kings and gentiles and homemakers and dentists and plumbers and schoolchildren.

I was saved into a midsized Baptist church, suburban in its sentiments, conservative in its theology. It was a world both familiar and strange to me. The music was awful, third-rate lyrics set to fourth-rate melodies, as C. S. Lewis is said to have described the music at his Anglican church. The preaching was interminable and often bewildering, an exercise in splitting hairs over doctrinal points that, until then, I knew nothing about. We signed a member's "covenant" to the effect that we wouldn't drink and wouldn't chew and wouldn't go with those who do.

But I loved it. I was taught the Bible, rote teaching methods notwithstanding, and soon enough I could split a doctrinal hair as thin and fine as the next guy. I even started to like the bad church music. But even more, I came to a deeper and deeper awareness of the gift of God, vouchsafed me by no merit of my own: that Christ died for me and lives in me and prepares a place for me. I am a new creation, heaven-bent. I am an enemy of God who has been made his child and his ambassador by the Father's grace and Christ's work and the Spirit's quickening.

Yet I look out week upon week on the congregation I now lead and wonder: Is the gospel I inherited, and now preach, too small? Is there a stump where an oak once stood? I wonder.

The conversions I witness generally aren't as radical as they seem to be elsewhere and at other times. Our hunger and thirst for righteousness, the first mark of kingdom dwellers, is for the most part anorexic, and our lust for self-vindication appears as hearty as ever. Domestic problems seem to be as prevalent among evangelicals as they are among the wider public. The amount of interchurch migration, and the low level of actual net church growth, is embarrassing. The willingness, as the apostle Paul put it, to share in the fellowship of Christ's sufferings so that we might attain to the resurrection from the dead is at a low ebb in most North American churches.

LONGING TO BE FREE

Let's go back to the early days of the church, when the Good News was new news. Let's go back to a jail in the city of Philippi, to two men sitting in the inner cell, bound in manacles. Paul and Silas. They're bleeding. Their flesh blooms with welts bright as red roses, bruises dark as purple dahlias. And they're singing.

I always picture them singing a Wesley tune—"And Can It Be," let's say—but know that's impossible. So maybe they sang the hymn Paul taught the Philippians: Let your attitude be the same as that of Christ Jesus . . . who became in very nature a servant.[55]

The point is, they're singing. And the gospel is doing its subversive, transforming work. Before the day's out (actually, this happens around midnight, so before it's barely begun), the jailer is on his knees, shaking from stem to stern, begging those two men, "Sirs, what must I do to be saved?"[56]

Their answer is beautiful in its clarity and brevity: "Believe in the Lord Jesus, and you will be saved—you and your household."[57]

Good News. The gospel. Just like I heard it, and embraced it, over twenty-five years ago.

I never want to make the gospel more complicated than that. I want to retain this gospel's deep simplicity for all time. Saved can never mean less than the forgiveness of sins and the hope of eternal life through faith in Christ.

But I wonder if God meant it to be more than this as well. The question that intrigues me is this: What did that jailer understand by the word *saved*? What did he want to convert to? What did he see in Paul and Silas that he himself lacked and now longed for?

Now it's possible that the jailer, like Nicodemus talking in the night with Jesus about rebirth, like the Samaritan woman at the well talking with Jesus about living water, is just confused. It's possible that his question and Paul's answer are miles apart—that all the jailer means is, "How do I get myself out of this mess?" and Paul seizes the moment to preach salvation.

It's possible, but I don't think so. I believe the jailer has been listening and watching and calculating all night long. I think Paul and Silas embody something he is afraid to believe "because of joy and amazement."[58] I think Paul and Silas are to him what all Christians are to be to the world: the fragrance of Christ.

SINGING AMID DISASTER

Consider four things.

First, the jailer saw two men counting it all joy when they faced trials of many kinds, men praying and singing in the face of bodily affliction and personal injustice that would have left most men howling and cursing. Paul and Silas, without due process, were stripped naked and "severely flogged" in public. The Romans had a special genius for this kind of thing (think of the flogging scene in the movie *The Passion of the Christ*). It was brutal torture joined to abject humiliation. The beating would scar or even maim them for life. Paul and Silas were summarily tossed in prison, locked in the inner cell, their feet put in stocks. Roman stocks were designed not just as extra security measures, but as implements of torture.

How would I respond? I wonder. How might you? Here's what they did: "About midnight Paul and Silas were praying and singing hymns to God, and the other prisoners were listening to them."[59]

Listening indeed! Who among them had ever witnessed such peculiar people, singing and praying in the face of colossal personal disaster? Who had ever heard of a God who, seemingly absent from or indifferent to these men's suffering, nevertheless called forth from them such pure devotion?

In 2006, five Amish girls, ages six to thirteen, were shot and killed by a man in Lancaster County, Pennsylvania, who then killed himself. The event stunned the world. But what happened next stunned the world all the more: a whole community singing and praying. A whole community not bent on retaliation, not shouting with anger or collapsing in despair, but standing with quiet dignity and deep calm. The community was quick to forgive. They even established a charity fund for the killer's family. We saw a people face the worst and become their best.

Such peculiar people.

The prisoners and, I think, the jailer witnessed two men like that. And he and they must have understood "saved" to mean, at the least, having confidence in a God who is with us and for us even when it looks as though he's abandoned us or is punishing us. It means knowing this God so personally that we have cause to sing even when there is no earthly reason to warrant it.

When we suffer, God empowers us to face the worst and become our best.

WE'RE ALL HERE

Somewhere in there, the jailer falls asleep. Maybe the singing lulls him. But he's awakened abruptly by a mighty shaking. An earthquake, powerful enough to fling the prison doors wide, strong enough to shake the prisoners' chains loose, rocks the house. The jailer wakes, sees what's happened, and prepares to do what every loyal Roman soldier knows is the noble thing to do: kill himself. Run his sword through his own heart to save Caesar's representative the trouble. A jailbreak was grounds for executing the prison guard regardless of the circumstances under which the prisoners escaped.

"But Paul shouted, 'Don't harm yourself! We are all here!'" This moment more than any other elicits the jailer's pleading question: "What must I do to be saved?"[60]

This is the point at which the jailer might mean by "saved" something very different from what Paul answers, but it's more likely that he's astonished by what he sees: these men's compassion for him, a stranger, even an enemy. Why should Paul and Silas care? What possible concern is it of theirs if this man does his soldierly duty? That earthquake looks like a God-thing, reminiscent of Peter's miraculous, angel-escorted escape from prison (where the guards were executed), reminiscent of the earthquake that attended Jesus' escape from death's prison. So why not see it as God's intervention on their behalf, and whatever will be will be?

Don't harm yourself. We're all here.

Such peculiar people. What power could possibly make anyone behave this way? What power is now loose in the cosmos that could break anyone's addiction to self-protection and self-advancement and make them care, even at great personal cost, about someone they've no reason to like and every reason to hate?

Suffering enables us to know that God empowers us—even when it costs us dearly—to love strangers, even enemies.

TRANSFIXED

Then there are the other prisoners, sitting there when nothing external—no chains, no bars—holds them any more. We're all here.

Why don't they flee? What's riveted them to their seats?

I venture this: Paul and Silas have astonished the prisoners every bit as much as they've astonished the jailer, and for the same reasons. Up to this moment, it's unlikely that a single one of those prisoners had ever seen a man get bludgeoned half to death and come up praising God. They're transfixed by it, wondering what strange power this is that causes men to act at complete odds with common sense. They're so transfixed, they start acting that way, too.

The jailer sees prisoners going nowhere. He sees prisoners who, hours before, would have seized this opportunity gleefully, without a second thought, now sitting still. If they are not as concerned about the jailer's welfare as Paul and Silas are, they at least respect Paul and Silas enough to follow their example. The guard sees hard men with hard hearts suddenly acting against their most entrenched instincts, and all because they eavesdropped for an hour or so on two men deeply in love with God.

God often uses suffering to soften and subdue the hardest heart.

And maybe there's one other thing that the jailer means by "saved." Maybe he knows what happened in town that day, the events that led to Paul and Silas being beaten and arrested and imprisoned. Maybe he knows that these two men are no criminals. That their crime is not murder or thievery or sedition, but simply and only setting a captive free.

Paul and Silas are in prison because they had pity on a slave girl, doubly enslaved, held in thrall by her earthly masters and the devil. She followed Paul and Silas around town, giving them one doozy of an endorsement: "These men are servants of the Most High God, who are telling you the way to be saved."[61]

She spoke the truth, every word. And her endorsement could only have helped Paul's cause tremendously: she was a local "spiritual authority," sought for her clairvoyance, her insight into hidden things. By all appearances, the foreign spirit in her was subject to the Holy Spirit of God.

Still, there was a foreign spirit in her. And it troubled Paul. So, in the name of Jesus, he cast the spirit out. As so often happens in the Gospels and Acts, when all heaven breaks loose, all hell does as well. The incident provokes a riot, and the result is that Paul and Silas exchange their freedom for hers. She's free, at least from the prison of the evil one, and they're captive, at least in the prison of the state.

Knowing that God defeats the powers of darkness enables us to bear suffering and become willing to forsake our own freedom and comfort for the sake of another's.

GLIMPSING TRANSFORMATION

What must I do to be saved?

Believe in Jesus. Yes. Believe in Jesus, so that your sins will be forgiven and your name written in the Book of Life. Please, let us never, in the name of any fashion or fad in theology, make the gospel less than this.

But what do we mean, what should we mean, by "saved"? Does it not also include freedom and power, here and now, to live a life so transformed that others glimpse in it the possibility of their own transformation? Please, let us always, in the name of the God who saves us, mean this by the gospel as well.

Arthur Burns, a Jewish economist of great influence in Washington during the tenure of several Presidents, was once asked to pray at a gathering of evangelical politicians. Stunning his hosts, he prayed thus: "Lord, I pray that Jews would come to know Jesus Christ. And I pray that Buddhists would come to know Jesus Christ. And I pray that Muslims would come to know Jesus Christ."

And then, most stunning of all: "And Lord, I pray that Christians would come to know Jesus Christ."[62]

Such a good prayer, I've started praying it myself.

PART IV

TRAVELING LIGHT

If you're planning a backpack trek through the wilderness, step one is to gather everything you might need and heap it on the kitchen table.

Step two is to get rid of half of what you've gathered.

Step three is to get rid of half of that.

When you realize that everything you want to take along on your two or three days of hiking will be borne along on two straps digging into your shoulder muscles, it makes you a little more judicious about what you stuff into that backpack. (Do you really need that iron skillet and your exhaustive concordance?) It might be difficult to leave potentially useful things behind, but somewhere along that two-thousand-foot elevation gain, walking into a stiff wind, you may be very glad that you did. In fact, you'll enjoy the views and vistas all the more when your shoulders are lighter.

Life can be like that too. Many of us have a tendency to go too fast and carry too much. Scripture, however, tells us to walk in the Spirit (not sprint or run), and to daily cast all our cares on Jesus, who cares for us.[63] We might fool ourselves by thinking that the more we carry, the more we are weighted down and weary, the more we are accomplishing and pleasing the Lord.

In fact, the very opposite might be true.

In this section, Ruth Haley Barton, Gordon MacDonald, and Mark Buchanan offer timely (and welcome) counsel, showing us how to slow down . . . and lighten up.

12

A STEADY RHYTHM

———— ◉ ————

The Not-So-Secret Key to Effective
Ministry and Leadership

RUTH HALEY BARTON

At a staff meeting in a church I was serving, we were discuss-ing how we could attract more people to join the church and increase their involvement. Someone did the math and pointed out that there were already at least five time commitments per week expected of those who wanted to become church members!

Outwardly I tried to be supportive of the meeting's purpose, but on the inside I was screaming, who would want to sign up for this? I was already trying to combat CFS (Christian Fatigue Syndrome) in my own life and couldn't imagine willingly inflicting it on someone else.

How is it that life in and around the church often gets reduced to so much activity, so much busyness, such incessant expectations? Without adequate time for rest, we lose the ability to be fully present.

As I looked around the planning table that day, I realized one of the main reasons church life is full of so much activity and busyness: this is the way its leaders are living.

Most of us know only one speed: full steam ahead. And we have been stuck in that speed for a very long time. If we do not establish saner rhythms in our own lives—life patterns that curb our unbridled activism and calm our compulsive busyness—we will not make it over the long haul. And neither will the people we are leading!

WORK HARD, REST FAITHFULLY

Jesus understood how quickly our passions, even the most noble, can wear us out if we're not careful. Early in his ministry with the disciples, he began to teach them about the importance of establishing sane rhythms of work and rest.

In Mark 6, Jesus commissioned the disciples for ministry and gave them the authority to cast out demons, to preach the gospel, and to heal the sick. They went off on their first ministry excursion and returned all excited about their newfound power and influence. They crowded around Jesus to report all they had done.

But what does Jesus do? He didn't seem to have much time for their ministry reports. Immediately he instructed them, "Come with me privately to an isolated place and rest a while."[64] He seemed more concerned about helping them establish a rhythm that would sustain them in ministry rather than allowing them to be overly enamored by ministry success, which can lead to a compulsion to do more and more without ceasing.

When we keep pushing forward without taking adequate time for rest, our way of life may seem heroic, but there is a frenetic quality to our work that lacks true effectiveness because we lose the ability to be fully present. Present to God and present to other people. And we lose the ability to discern what is really needed in our situation.

The result can be "sloppy desperation," a mental and spiritual state in which we're just trying to get it all done. And this prevents us from the quality of presence that delivers true insight and spiritual leadership.

Charles, a gifted physician, illustrates the point: "I discovered in medical school that if I saw a patient when I was tired or overworked, I would order a lot of tests. I was so exhausted, I couldn't tell exactly what was going on, so I got in the habit of ordering a battery of tests, hoping they would tell me what I was missing.

"But when I was rested, if I had the opportunity to get some sleep or go for a quiet walk, then when I saw the next patient, I could rely on my intuition and experience to give me an accurate reading of what was happening. When I could take the time to listen and be present with them and their illness, I was almost always right."

When we are depleted, we become overly reliant on clamoring voices outside of us for direction. We react to symptoms rather than seeking to understand and respond to underlying causes. We rely on other people's ministry models because we are too tired to listen and observe our setting and craft something uniquely suited for this place.

When we are rested, we bring steady, alert attention to our leadership and are characterized by discernment of what is truly needed in our situation. And we have the energy and creativity to carry it out.

RHYTHMS OF ENGAGEMENT AND RETREAT

One of the most important rhythms for those of us in ministry is to establish a constant back-and-forth motion between engagement and retreat. We need regular times to engage in the battle, giving our best energy to the task. Then we need regular times when we step back to gain perspective, restrategize, and tend our wounds—an inevitability of life in ministry.

An occupational hazard for us in Christian ministry is that it can be hard to distinguish between the times we are "on," working for God, and times when we can just be with God to replenish our own soul. Our time with Scripture can be reduced to a textbook or a tool for ministry rather than an intimate communication from God to me personally. Even prayer can become an exhausting round of different kinds of mental activity, or a public display of our spiritual prowess.

Times of extended retreat give us a chance to come home to God's presence and to be open with God, in utter privacy, about what is true of us. This is important for us and for those we serve.

When we repress what is real in our lives and just keep soldiering on, we get weary from holding it in and eventually it leaks out in ways that are damaging to ourselves and to others. But on retreat there is time and space to attend to what is real in our own lives—to celebrate the joys, grieve the losses, shed tears, sit with our questions, feel our anger, attend to our loneliness—and allow God to be with us in those places.

These are not times for problem solving, because not everything can be fixed or solved. On retreat we rest ourselves in God and wait on him to do what is needed, and we return to the battle with fresh energy and keener insight.

SILENCE AND WORD

The writer of Proverbs tells us, "When words abound, transgression is inevitable."[65] This is a truth that can drive us ministry folks to despair given the incessant flow of words we feel compelled to issue from our mouths, pens, and computers. Those of us who deal in words are at great risk of misusing them and even sinning with our words due to the sheer volume of them!

I don't know about you, but sometimes I can literally feel it—deep in my bones—that if I do not shut my mouth for awhile, I will get myself in trouble because my words will be completely disconnected from the reality of God in my own life. Silence is the only cure for this desperate situation.

"Right speech comes out of silence, and right silence comes out of speech," wrote Dietrich Bonhoeffer. In silence our speech patterns are refined because silence fosters a self-awareness that enables us to choose more truly the words that we say.

Rather than speech that issues from our subconscious needs to impress, to put others in their place, to compete, control, and manipulate, to put a good spin on things, we are able to notice our inner dynamics and make choices that are more grounded in love, trust, and God-given wisdom.

The psalmist says, "When you are disturbed, do not sin; ponder it on your beds and be silent. Offer right sacrifices [in other words, stay faithful to your spiritual practices], and put your trust in the Lord."[66]

At times the most heroic thing you, as leader, can do is to remain in that private place with God for as long as it takes to consciously trust yourself to God rather than to everything else you could be doing in the moment.

STILLNESS AND ACTION

Practicing rhythms of silence and words, stillness and action, helps us learn to wait on God—which doesn't come easily for those of us accustomed to busily trying to make things happen. It takes energy to be restrained, to wait for the work of God in our lives and in the situations we face.

But the more I am called upon to use words, the more distressing things are, the more active leadership that is required of me—the more silence I need.

It is an embarrassing little secret, common among leaders, and we need to be more honest about it: buried deep in the psyche of many leaders is a Superman mentality—that somehow we are not like other human beings, and we can function beyond normal human limitations and save the world. Or at least our little corner of the world. This is a myth that we indulge to our own peril.

Sabbath keeping is the primary discipline that helps us live within the limits of our humanity and to honor God as our Creator. It is the key to a life lived in sync with the rhythms that God himself built into our world. Yet it is the discipline that seems hardest for us to live.

Sabbath keeping honors the body's need for rest, the spirit's need for replenishment, and the soul's need to delight itself in God for God's own sake.

It begins with the willingness to acknowledge the limits of our humanness and then to take steps to begin to live more graciously within the order of things.

And the first order of things is that we are creatures and God is the creator. God is the only one who is infinite; I, on the other hand, must learn to live within the physical limits of time and space and the human limits of strength and energy.

There are limits to my relational, emotional, mental, and spiritual capacities as well. I am not God. God is the only one who can be all things to all people. God is the only one who can be two places at once. God is the one who never sleeps. I am not.

This is pretty basic stuff, but many of us live as though we don't know it.

Sabbath keeping may be the most challenging rhythm for leaders to establish because Sunday, in most churches, has become a day of Christian busyness—perhaps the busiest! And, of course, the busiest person on that day is the pastor!

This just means that pastors need to set aside another day for their Sabbath. Or they might consider ordering their church's life so that everyone learns how to practice Sabbath. It could begin with worship, but then everyone goes home and rests and delights for the rest of the day because there are no other church activities. In that way, the pastor's commitment to Sabbath becomes a blessing for everyone.

Sabbath keeping is a way of ordering one's whole life to honor the rhythm of things—work and rest, fruitfulness and dormancy, giving and receiving, being and doing, activism and surrender. The day itself is set apart, devoted completely to rest, worship, and delighting in God and his good gifts. And the rest of the week must be lived in such a way as to make Sabbath possible.

There is something deeply spiritual about honoring the limitations of our human existence. We are physical and spiritual beings in a world of time and space. A peace descends upon us when we accept what is real rather than always pushing beyond our limits. By being gracious, accepting, and gentle with ourselves at least once a week, we're enabled to be gracious, accepting, and gentle with others.

There is a freedom that comes from being who we are in God and resting into God. This eventually enables us to bring something truer to the world than all of our striving.

Sabbath keeping helps us to live within our limits because on the Sabbath, in so many different ways, we allow ourselves to be the creature in the presence of our Creator. We touch something more real than what we are able to produce on our own. We touch our very being in God.

Surely that is what the people around us need most.

13

THE CRUCIAL NEED FOR REGULAR REST

———— ◉ ————

One of God's Underused Gifts Is Time to Be Sharpened

GORDON MACDONALD

Once, when my wife, Gail, and I were hiking the Swiss Alps' high meadows, we saw two farmers cutting the high-standing mountain grasses with scythes, a hand-mowing tool that has been around since ancient times. Their broad-sweeping movements seemed like the synchronous movements of dancers.

Drawing closer, we noticed that both paused periodically and produced from their pockets something resembling a flat stone. Then in the same graceful manner, they drew the stones back and forth across the scythes' blades. The purpose? To restore sharpness.

The sharpening done, each returned to the cutting.

Gail and I observed them repeat this process—cut and sharpen, cut and sharpen—several times: ten minutes (give or take) of cutting followed by five minutes of sharpening.

A dumb question: why waste five minutes sharpening the blades? We're talking here about twenty minutes of unproductive time each hour. Why not keep cutting, get the job finished, and head home at an earlier hour?

Answer: because with every swing of the scythe, the blade

becomes duller. And with the increasing dullness, the work becomes harder and less productive. Result: you actually head home much later.

Lesson learned: cutting and sharpening are both part of a farmer's work.

Lesson applied: In my earliest pastoral years, I didn't appreciate this cutting/sharpening principle. I'm embarrassed to admit that I usually gave attention to the sharpening (or the spiritual) dimension of my life only when I needed something beyond my natural reach or when I found myself knee-deep in trouble.

The cumulative results of a life lived like this became alarming. It led to dullness of the soul.

While talking a lot about God, I had very little practice in listening to him.

My work fell prey to mission-creep. I tended to become bogged down in matters of secondary importance, neglecting truly important things.

I often complained of fatigue: not only physical fatigue, but spiritual and emotional emptiness.

Sometimes I became flooded with temptations to envy, impatience, ambition, discontent, wandering thoughts.

I was too sensitive, easily rattled by criticism, disagreement, and the slights of people who seemed not to be on my side.

I often did not feel I was doing my best. I seemed to give God and people a B-minus effort.

My prayers were shallow, not reflective of a man who was supposed to "walk with God."

While most people complimented me as a good preacher and pastor, the fact was that I was not influencing many people toward a deeper commitment to Jesus Christ.

As time passed and I hit one too many "walls," I began an earnest search for what was missing at the center of my life. If I could not identify it, I feared that I was not going to last. It was then I discovered a most important biblical law: Sabbath—holy time when the soul is sharpened.

Somehow the Sabbath idea had not come alive to me before. I perceived Sabbath as a wild Sunday of spellbinding preaching, growing crowds, and successful programming. I never imagined a Sabbath experience of majestic worship, joyful quiet (instead of noise), interior "conversation," and a reordering of the pieces of my life. No wonder I felt so messy. I knew none of these.

All this is the result of a widespread reluctance to take God seriously when he says there are times when work in the world must stop (really, really stop!) and be replaced by work in the soul.

Imagine what a Sabbath pause might look like. There would be twenty-four hours of relative quiet in which to escape the unrelenting busyness in order to listen to God; twenty-four hours of intimacy with those one loves the most; twenty-four hours to appraise the recent days and count one's blessings and resolve one's regrets; twenty-four hours to look forward and reorder one's priorities and sense of direction; twenty-four hours to reaffirm true belief and obedience to God the Creator; twenty-four hours to rest, laugh, study, and play.

Simply imagining it causes me to breathe deeply and ask: What keeps me from this?

I was in my early thirties when this Sabbath-sharpening idea began to make sense. And it started not with Protestant or Catholic sources but by acquainting myself with Jewish thinkers.

Author and playwright Herman Wouk, an observant Jew, describes in his book, *This Is My God*, his life of faith and makes it clear that the Sabbath was at the core of his way of life.

STRENGTH, REFRESHMENT, AND CHEER

"I can now tell (the reader)," Wouk wrote, "that (the Sabbath) day is the fulcrum of a practicing Jew's existence and generally a source of strength, refreshment, and cheer." That line certainly caught my attention.

"The great difference between the Puritan Sabbath and the even more restrictive Jewish *Shabbat* is an impalpable but overwhelming one of spirit. Our Sabbath opens with blessings over light and wine. Light and wine are the keys to the day. Our observance has its solemnities, but *the main effect is release, peace, gaiety, and lifted spirits*" (emphasis mine).[67]

Reread Wouk's last four descriptors. When was the last time you ended a Protestant Sabbath (Sunday) and described yourself in such a fashion?

Wouk went on to describe a typical Sabbath in his Jewish family. Each week he arrived home—a New York City apartment—by sundown on Friday night.

"Leaving the gloomy theater [where Wouk worked], the littered coffee cups, the jumbled scarred-up scripts, the haggard actors, the shouting stagehands, the bedeviled director, the knuckle-gnawing producer, the clattering typewriter, and the dense tobacco smoke and the backstage dust, I have come home. It has been a startling change, very much like a brief return from the wars."[68]

Notice the description of the theater and its echo of the larger world in which he (and we) live. And then notice the ordered world found in his home.

His wife and his boys awaited his arrival. Soon after the family sat down to a splendid dinner "at a table graced with flowers and the Sabbath symbols."[69] Then—and I love this—Wouk touches each of his sons and blesses them. All of this is followed by eating, singing, conversation, and prepared questions. "For me," Wouk says, "[Sabbath] is a retreat into restorative magic."[70]

Restorative magic: what a term.

Saturday, Wouk adds, is passed in much the same manner. There is a synagogue gathering and the embrace of the worshipping community. There is play in the park. There is togetherness. "On the Sabbath," he says, "[our boys know that] we are always there. . . . They know too that I am not working, and that my wife is at her ease. It is their day."[71]

"It is my day too," Wouk writes. "The telephone [think Blackberry or iPhone here] is silent. I can think, read, study, walk, or do nothing. It is an oasis of quiet."[72]

When Wouk returns to the theater on Saturday night after Sabbath has ended, someone says to him, "I don't envy you your religion, but I envy you your Sabbath."[73]

Rabbi Jonathan Sacks, in his book, *Faith in the Future*, writes not dissimilarly about his Sabbath: "Imagine the experience of coming home on Friday afternoon. The week has flown by in a rush of activity. You are exhausted. And there, in all its simplicity and splendor is the Sabbath table: candles radiating the light that symbolizes *shalom bayit*, peace at 'home; wine, representing blessing and joy; and two loaves of bread, recalling the double portion of manna that fell for the Israelites in the wilderness so that they would not have to gather food on the seventh day."[74]

Then, get this. "Seeing that table you know that until tomorrow evening you will step into another world, one where there are no pressures to work or compete or distractions or interruptions, just time to be together with family and friends."[75]

Come to think of it, no one that I remember ever envied my Sabbath. Maybe it was because I had no consistent or well-ordered personal sharpening experience for anyone to envy.

An elder in one of my congregations once said to me at the end of a long, very busy Sunday morning: "I'm sure glad that God only insisted on one Sabbath each week. If he'd required two, I'd have a nervous breakdown."

By contrast, Senator Joseph Lieberman, an observant Jew, writes in his book *The Gift of Rest*, "For me, Sabbath observance is a gift because it is one of the deepest, purest pleasures in my life. It is a day of peace, rest, and sensual pleasure."[76]

Explaining that last phrase, Lieberman writes: "When I said the Sabbath is sensual, I meant that it engages the senses—sight, sound, taste, smell, and touch—with beautiful settings, soaring melodies, wonderful food and wine, and lots of love. It is a time to reconnect with family and friends . . . with God, the Creator of everything we have time to 'sense' on the Sabbath. Sabbath observance is a gift that has anchored, shaped, and inspired my life."[77]

Is there anything about the way most of us Protestants and Catholics "do church" these days that can be likened to what Wouk, Sacks, and Lieberman have said?

In my younger days of inner disorganization, the nagging question became: If God intends there to be experiences of release, peace, gaiety, a lifted spirit—then how can I experience them?

I wish I could answer this question by telling you that I regularly take full twenty-four-hour Sabbaths. That would be untruthful. But I have learned to insert genuine Sabbath "sharpenings" into my life even if they have usually been briefer than twenty-four hours.

THE PERSONAL SIDE OF SABBATH

There are two sides to Sabbath: the personal side and the communal or public side where one engages with friends and congregation.

Here I want to reflect on the first of the two. In our home over the past many years, the starting point for each day has been a Sabbath-silence. We have learned the value of time in a private place. No noise, no interruptions, no distractions. In the past, when there were children in our home, we simply arranged to find this time in morning's earliest hours before they awakened. This, of course, meant going to bed earlier. And it actually worked for us.

Over the years I have come to guard those quiet moments as among my most precious treasures. Each morning the time is spent differently. But the goal is always the same. Again to quote Herman Wouk: "to find release, peace, gaiety, and lifted spirits." The larger purpose? To prepare to walk through the coming day obedient to Jesus, useful to people, embedded (not insulated) fully in the larger world.

Thomas à Kempis said of reflective moments: "Be faithful to your secret place, and it will become your closest friend and bring you much comfort. In silence and stillness a devout person grows spiritually and learns the hidden things of the Bible. Tears shed there bring cleansing. God draws near to the one who withdraws for a while. It is better for you to look after yourself this way in private than to perform wonders in public while neglecting your soul."

In these private Sabbaths, I have found a number of activities that are essential to my own day-to-day sharpening. They are my spiritual version of the sharpening of the farmer's scythe.

Vigorous Repentance. I must start here because repentance is life saving and heaven opening. I once thought that repentance simply meant that when you do something bad, you mention it, say that you're sorry, and move on. But a revisiting of the Bible on this subject has moved me to understand that repentance is, first and foremost, an acknowledgement of that deeper pool of evil that lies resident in every one of us and which is ready to explode at any moment.

What a noisy life I live. How many unfinished thoughts fly away, never to be remembered again. A deeper repentance means that I must examine my heart for such potential waywardness and renounce the tendency to compare myself with others, to explain away my failures, and to whine if someone isn't merciful to me.

Repentance means that I have to present myself to God and speak the equivalent of Isaiah's words, "Woe is me; I am a broken man."[78] This has required a painful humility, a regular readjustment. There remain many moments when a rebellious part of me still tries to avoid owning and assessing my own messiness (active and potential). The Sabbath experience—the sharpening of the blade—means this cannot be avoided.

Immersion in the Bible. Each day I push myself to read it not as a preacher preparing talks for others, but as one hungry (sometimes desperate) for God's kind and searching words.

I confess an unbridled love of the Bible's stories, especially those of Jesus and his disciples.

There are life-long favorite places such as the oft-read Psalm 23. I often sit quietly and repeat this Psalm over and over again. With each repetition, I pause and contemplate individual words: cool waters . . . darkened valleys . . . rods, staffs . . . banqueting tables . . . the qualities of goodness and mercy (what powerful words to a sinner like me). I love to imagine the great shepherd, Jesus himself, going before me: urging calmness in those green pastures, assuring me of his presence amid danger, swabbing my wounds with oil, serving me a healthy dinner while my "enemies" look on, powerless to do anything.

Reading the Great Spiritual Masters. I'd never had time for those strange folk when I was young. But now I read them with great appreciation: Augustine, Lawrence, Fenelon, Fox, Thomas à Kempis.

They speak to my soul. Quakers, Catholics, Puritans, monks, mystics. Each brings a fresh perspective and builds in me a balance of understanding of this immense God who will not be fully captured by any one tradition or theological perspective.

Reflection. What a noisy life I have lived. How many unfinished thoughts have flown through my mind never to be remembered again? How many experiences have gone unevaluated in the past? How many times did I fail to take inventory of the day and squeeze events and conversations that might morph into wisdom? How often have I forgotten to express thanks? Reflection is the act of gathering these things and squeezing meaning and message out of them.

Journaling. Among the most important daily exercises I ever undertook was the day (December 17, 1968) when I began describing myself on the pages of a notebook. Over the years these journals have included records of each day's experiences where I heard (or missed) God's voice, what was delightful or regrettable. My journals include prayers, quotes, Bible references, and comments made to me by "angels" in the course of the day. Just as Israel built memorials to God's great acts and revelations, so my journals have been a memorial to God's grace in my life.

Worship. In Sabbath one must kneel before the Lord, assume that prayerful posture, and reaffirm once again the words: "Worship the Lord with gladness; come before him with joyful songs. Know that the LORD is God. It is he who made us, and we are his; we are his people, the sheep of his pasture."[79]

In the act of worship—exalting God's character, his mighty acts, and reliable promises—we are appropriately upsized or downsized, depending on who we think we are at the moment. More than once I have been painfully reduced to true size by a God who will not tolerate my self-centeredness. Then there have been times when I have been so low and this wonderfully gracious God has lifted me out of "that slimy pit" and filled me with a new song.

Sabbath Imagining. It's often unappreciated, but the heavenly Father has provided us an imagination (an inner theatrical stage, if you please) where we can visualize scenarios of possible futures for ourselves. The long future (what sort of man might I be in ten years?) and the short one (for what must I prepare today?).

During my Sabbath moments, I quietly dream through the conversations I am scheduled to have. I often think about the tasks that populate my to-do list. As I imagine, I ask questions: How could I be useful in that situation? What might I say if he or she . . .? Can I be a better listener? What word from God might come through me? It is in these imagining moments that God's Holy Spirit paints possibilities on our minds.

And so it is with my Sabbaths. The inner blade is sharpened, and one reenters the larger world with greater focus and spiritual energy.

I love the words of Rufus Jones, a biographer of George Fox, founder of the Quaker movement: "In all his planning and arrangements he exalted the place of hush and silence, and he taught his followers to prize the times of quiet meditation in their gatherings for worship, so that he left behind him a fellowship of persons who knew how to cultivate the interior deeps within themselves and who had discovered how to make their own approach to God without external helps."

Along with Gail and me, George Fox would have loved those Swiss farmers.

14

STRIVING FOR SIMPLICITY

———— ◉ ————

Breaking Free from the Cult of the Next Thing

MARK BUCHANAN

I belong to the Cult of the Next Thing. It's dangerously easy to get enlisted. It happens by default—not by choosing the cult, but by failing to resist it. The Cult of the Next Thing is consumerism cast in religious terms. It has its own litany of sacred words: more, you deserve it, new, faster, cleaner, brighter. It has its own deep-rooted liturgy: charge it, instant credit, no down payment, deferred payment, no interest for three months. It has its own preachers, evangelists, prophets, and apostles: ad men, pitchmen, celebrity sponsors. It has, of course, its own shrines, chapels, temples, meccas: malls, superstores, club warehouses. It has its own sacraments: credit and debit cards. It has its own ecstatic experiences: the spending spree.

Most of us spend more time with advertisements than with Scripture.

The Cult of the Next Thing's central message proclaims, "Crave and spend, for the Kingdom of Stuff is here." Sanctification is measured by never saving enough: for the cult teaches that our lives are measured by the abundance of our possessions. Those caught up in the Cult of the Next Thing live endlessly, relentlessly for, well, the

Next Thing—the next weekend, the next vacation, the next purchase, the next experience. For us, the impulse to seek the Next Thing is an instinct bred into us so young it seems genetic. It's our paradigm, our way of seeing. It's our unifying myth. How could the world be otherwise?

For Christians, this is a problem. The problem is ethical, spiritual, theological. And, of course, practical. The one time Jesus got violent was when the temple had been made into a marketplace. Jesus brooked a lot of things with uncanny calmness—demoniacs yelling at him, religious leaders plotting against him, thick-headed, slow-hearted disciples bossing him. But moneychangers and holy-trinket sellers put a wildness in him. And lest we miss the object lesson, Jesus puts his opposition to the Cult of the Next Thing in plain speech:

> No one can serve two masters. For you will hate one and love the other; you will be devoted to one and despise the other. You cannot serve both God and money. That is why I tell you not to worry about everyday life—whether you have enough food and drink, or enough clothes to wear. . . . These things dominate the thoughts of unbelievers, but your heavenly Father already knows all your needs.[80]

Paul also had a thing or two to say about the cult:

> People who long to be rich fall into temptation and are trapped by many foolish and harmful desires that plunge them into ruin and destruction. For the love of money is the root of all kinds of evil. And some people, craving money, have wandered from the true faith and pierced themselves with many sorrows.[81]

We know all this, but simply knowing it doesn't usually help. The cult is big, powerful, well organized, flawlessly run. It is so dominating it can usurp almost any impulse—even the impulse toward simplicity: You can package it, market it, and make a profit off of it. It renders even its enemies into minions, turns even protests against it into pithy slogans. In the late nineties, a whole range of ads—from cars to clothes to CD players—traded on a growing resentment against commercialism. Forty-thousand-dollar sports utility vehicles were touted as the magic means of escaping the artificiality of a world locked into work and shopping. These ads were put together without any hint of irony.

NO SATISFACTION

I am writing this on a computer I bought a little over a year ago. Then, it was one of the most powerful and advanced machines available to the ordinary consumer. Now, a year and some months later, it is, by industry standards, sluggish and clumsy, unable to handle the latest innovation in software.

But here's the real problem: all that bothers me. I look, every week, at the fliers from computer and electronics superstores and see computers more powerful, with greater speed and bigger monitors and much more memory—and for considerably less money than I paid—and it bothers me. I feel cheated. I feel saddled with a clunker. I wonder: Should I upgrade? Should I trade up? Yet here I sit, the words popping up as fast as I type them, amenable, at the stroke of a key or the click of a mouse, to all kinds of effortless manipulation—cut-and-paste, deletion or duplication, spelling and grammar checks, graphic enhancements. I have scores of fonts and pictures, and if that doesn't please me, I can pull up endless more from CDs or the Internet.

This computer will play music while I work. It can answer my phone. It can link me to the resource catalog of the New York Public Library. I can shop for just about anything, pay for it, and have it delivered, all without leaving my chair. This computer talks to me—a lovely, slightly seductive female voice, perfectly pitched between a business tone and an intimate one. I have a microphone, and if I could figure out how it worked, I could talk to this computer. This machine is more than I'll ever need. It is, in truth, more than I'll ever use: whole sections of its labyrinthine workings are *terra incognita* to me, a Middle Earth of the grotesque and the exotic.

But every week the fliers come, and this computer doesn't seem enough.

I told you, I belong to the Cult of the Next Thing. If ever there was a cult that gave us stones when we asked for bread, this is it. It promises so much. Look at the ads. If you get this car, take that trip, buy these clothes, use this detergent—what joy! What fulfillment will finally and fully be yours!

One of the strangest ads I ever saw was a television commercial for Kool-Aid. It showed a bunch of kids sitting slumped and sullen on a gorgeous summer day. They're bored, numbed with it. It's almost a portrait of suicidal despair. Why go on living? Then the mother brings out a round, dew-beaded pitcher of Kool-Aid, ruby red and jiggling with ice. The kids go crazy. They leap, they clap, they cheer, they run, they gulp. This, yes this, is something to live for! The impression we're given is that the exuberance over that moment lives long past the moment: that there is something redemptive about the pitcher of Kool-Aid, that it restores purpose and hope to all of life. Well, my own children like Kool-Aid. Just not that much.

THE SILENCE OF SIMPLICITY

I'm working on the discipline of ignoring the god of Next Things, of dropping out of that cult. What helps best is to cultivate a substitute discipline. I practice simplicity.

I built a shed this past summer. My garden equipment—shovels and rakes, a fertilizer broadcaster, a lawn mower, hoses, and sprinklers—was aging and rusting too quickly leaning against the house. And someone kept stealing my gas can. So I decided I needed a shed. I went down to the building supply store in town. The cheapest one—emphasis on cheap—was $500. That was too much. But while I was looking at one store, I noticed a large lot of cedar two-by-fours being cleared out—six hundred feet for fifty dollars. I bought it, and went home and framed up the shed. It sat, skeletal, for several weeks. Then a friend offered me the sheeting board to cover its exterior; he had bought a lot of wood on clearance the year before and wasn't going to use the sheeting.

Over the next month, I scavenged. Driving by a house that had just been built, I noticed that several bundles of unused shingles and a partial roll of tarpaper sat in the side lot. I tracked down the contractor and made a deal. I got them for half price. I found an old door and some planks for shelving in the crawl space at the church. And so it went: foraging, salvaging, bartering, scrounging, improvising. In the end, I had a great shed. It cost about $300, but I recently saw one like it in a catalog for $1,800.

In one sense, this wasn't simple. It took more time—a lot more—than if I had simply bought a kit and put it together in a day. Sometimes simplicity is just trading one complexity for another. But the time, most of it, was spent en route, as I went. It was more adventure than project. In the course of it, I had some good conversations, met some new people. My wife and children got the benefit of my childlike joy when I came home to announce, "You won't believe it. I've just been given all the batting for finishing the edges on the shed."

There's a deeper lesson here. In the midst of living this way, I have come to appreciate small things more.

I made a garden in the front of my house. I gathered all the elements—granite rock to edge it, soil, trees, flowers, driftwood—the same way I got the material for the shed. Because it took work—a dedication to simplicity doesn't always come simply—I delight in the color of the flowers. I see the bees flit from one to the next, and it gives me a deep-down satisfaction. Those bees are a signature of divine pleasure—God must like what I've done. I'm not sure I would think that—or even much notice the bees—if I had paid a landscaper to do the work.

But sometimes simplicity means forsaking the garden for the wilderness. Nehemiah did that. He was willing to walk away from the luxuries of the lavish Persian court—the gardens and pools and palaces—to go live among the miseries of ramshackle Jerusalem, with its open sewers and piles of rubble. Why? God had put it in his heart.[82]

The quest for simplicity can lapse into legalism. It can decay into brittle, mirthless austerity, or puff itself up into heroic do-it-yourself-ism. And then it's as barren as the Cult of the Next Thing. I once spoke with a man who imposed on his family fasting from television for a year. He said it was terrible. His family still resents him for it.

Simplicity is something more, something other than just doing without or doing it yourself. Its essence is neither forsaking nor striving. Its essence, rather, is listening: What has God put in your heart? Simplicity is, once having discerned that, being content with it. Simplify it further: simplicity is being content with God.

Mammon is a good servant—obliging, gracious, versatile. As a servant, he's willing to be used for anything. He'll slum or hobnob, it doesn't matter.

I've used money for a holiday in Thailand, bought Thai silk, ridden an elephant, snorkeled amid schools of bright-colored fish. And I've used money to buy those sticky wax rings that seal toilets to drain pipes. Mammon was handy in both instances.

But Mammon makes a poor god—demanding, capricious, conniving. He's surly and brutish, rarely lets you sleep well or long. He is sometimes generous, in a fickle way, but has a well-practiced habit of depriving us of taking deep and lasting pleasure in his gifts: he brings with his gifts the sour aftertaste of ingratitude (it's not enough), or fear (it won't last), or insatiableness (I want more). Maybe this is the worst irony of the Cult of the Next Thing: It trains us, not to value things too much, but to value them too little. It teaches us to not cherish and enjoy anything. Otherwise, we might be content and not long for the Next Thing.

And this: Mammon outshouts God. It's hard to hear what God has put in your heart with Mammon roaring. I write this on an island between Vancouver Island and the British Columbia mainland. Earlier in the day, I walked along a forest trail and returned to my cabin along the shoreline. The greenness of the water, the clatter of stone and shell underfoot, the natural sculpture of driftwood—it is a gallery of art. I sat on a shelf of sandstone that sloped down to the water. The sandstone, with its pits and ridges where the water's persistence has pried loose embedded stones, resembled a rough lizard hide, hugely magnified. This is a place of good silence. There are sounds, but they are woven into the texture of air and earth and water. It is a place for listening.

Walking home, in early evening, I heard voices. They sounded near, but they weren't. They came from across a vast expanse of water, sweeping effortlessly, like herons skimming the water's surface, over the distance. The voices traveled that distance intact, the shades of inflection still in them, no echo blurring their edges. I heard every word.

Simplicity is like a silence. It is a place for listening to a Voice that otherwise we might never hear.

ENOUGH IS ENOUGH

After silence comes speaking. There are two sayings, plain sayings, that are helping me live into simple contentment with God and what God puts in my heart. The first is "thank you."

I was in Uganda, Africa several years ago, in a little township called Wairacka. Every Sunday evening, about one hundred Christians from the neighboring area would gather to worship. They met under a tin-roof lean-to that was set at the edge of a cornfield. They sat—when they did sit—on rough wood benches. The floor was dirt. The instruments were old. Some of the guitars didn't have all the strings. But could they worship! They made hell run for shelter when they got loose. There was one guy with us, a real stiff-backed, buttoned-down white boy who liked his worship staid and orderly and brief, and even he couldn't stand still: he was jumping, clapping, yelling out his hallelujahs.

One Sunday evening, the pastor asked if anyone had anything to share. A tall, willowy woman came to the front. She was plain fea-tured, but she was beautiful. "Oh, brothers and sisters, I love Jesus so much," she started.

"Tell us, sister! Tell us!" the worshipers shouted back.

"Oh, I love him so much, I don't know where to begin to tell you how good he is."

"Begin there, sister! Begin right there!"

"Oh," she said, "he is so good to me. I praise him all the time for how good he is to me. For three months, I prayed to the Lord for shoes. And look!" And at that the woman cocked up her leg so that we could see one foot. One very ordinary shoe covered it. "He gave me shoes. Hallelujah, he is so good." And the Ugandans clapped and yelled and shouted back, "Hallelujah!"

I didn't. I was devastated. I sat there hollowed out, hammered down. In all my life I had not once prayed for shoes. And in all my life I had not once thanked God for the many, many shoes I had.

As I later tried to sort that out, I looked at a lot of Scriptures about being thankful. I discovered that being thankful and experiencing the power and presence of Jesus Christ are tightly entwined. As we practice thankfulness, we experience more of God's transforming grace, God's thereness.

I looked again at 1 Thessalonians 5:18: "No matter what happens, always be thankful" (TLB). And then at Ephesians 5:20: "Always give thanks for everything to God" (TLB). And it came to me that the deepest theological concept is not the doctrine of the Incarnation, or the theories of Atonement, or the arguments for theodicy. Not views on premillennialism or supralapsarianism, nor ideas about tribulationism or dispensationalism. No, the deepest theological concept is thankfulness. Because to know God is to thank God. To worship God is to thank God. And to thank God in all things and for all things is to acknowledge that God is good, perfectly good, and perfectly just, and perfectly powerful—and that all things do work together for good for those who love God and have been called according to God's purposes.

Thankfulness is an act of subversion against the Cult of the Next Thing.

The other saying, like "thank you" both simple and hard, is "enough." In the Garden of Eden the first thing the serpent did was create in Adam and Eve a sense of scarcity. "Did God really say you must not eat the fruit from any of the trees in the garden?"[83]

God did say—commanded, in fact—that they "may freely eat the fruit of every tree in the garden—except the tree of the knowledge of good and evil. If you eat its fruit, you are sure to die."[84] The serpent's trick, then as now, is to turn this staggering abundance and gracious protection into frightening scarcity and bullying deprivation, the stinginess of a despot.

The serpent lied, and we got taken in. Now, despite the overwhelming evidence that we live amid overflowing abundance—abundant food, clothes, warmth, friends, things—we always feel it's not enough. We sense it's running out, it's insufficient. We live for the Next Thing.

There is an Indian parable about this. A guru had a disciple and was so pleased with the man's spiritual progress that he left him on his own. The man lived in a little mud hut. He lived simply, begging for his food. Each morning, after his devotions, the disciple washed his loincloth and hung it out to dry. One day, he came back to discover the loincloth torn and eaten by rats. He begged the villagers for another, and they gave it to him. But the rats ate that one too. So he got himself a cat. That took care of the rats, but now when he begged for his food he had to beg for milk for his cat as well. "This won't do," he thought. "I'll get a cow." So he got a cow and found he had to beg now for fodder. So he decided to till and plant the ground around his hut. But soon he found no time for contemplation, so he hired servants to tend his farm. But overseeing the labors became a chore, so he married to have a wife to help him. After a time, the disciple became the wealthiest man in the village.

The guru was traveling by there and stopped in. He was shocked to see that where once stood a simple mud hut there now loomed a palace surrounded by a vast estate, worked by many servants. "What is the meaning of this?" he asked his disciple.

"You won't believe this, sir," the man replied, "but there was no other way I could keep my loincloth."

I know this trap. Earlier, I held up my shed as an example of simplicity. But why did I build it? There was no other way I could keep my rakes and shovels, lawn mower, and gas can. This business of enough is slippery: the staked pit of legalism on one side, the quicksand of rationalization on the other. What is enough? I think I'm learning to live with enough, but what I call enough is staggering lavishness to most of the world.

A woman from a poor village in Bangladesh was visiting a Christian family in Toronto, and the morning after she arrived she looked out the kitchen window of the people's home.

"Who lives in that house?" she asked the woman from Toronto.

"Which house?"

"That one, right there."

"Oh, that. No one lives there. That's a 'house' for the car."

The woman from Bangladesh was nonplussed. "A house for the car," she kept saying. "A house for the car."

I picture that woman, looking out my kitchen window and seeing my garden shed, puzzled, saying again and again, "A house for the shovels. A house for the lawn mower."

We live in a culture of excess. A culture of more. A culture where we need to accumulate endlessly just to keep the loincloth. And the only way to break it is deliberately to lay hold of another way of seeing and living: we need an attitude of enough. G. K. Chesterton is widely quoted as saying, "There are two ways to get enough. One is to accumulate more and more. The other is to need less." The attitude of enough—actually, it's a spiritual orientation— is marked by trust, contentment, and thankfulness. It is the decision, without rationalization, to say, "This is enough. My home is big enough. My car is new enough. My possessions are plenty enough. I've eaten enough. I've taken enough. Enough is enough."

And when we begin to live out the spirituality of enough, there comes a point when we see that maybe we have more than enough.

JUST SAY NO

There is a lady I know who lives this way, thankful with enough. Her name is Helen, and she attends the church that I pastor. Helen is who I want to be when I grow up. She lives, as far as I can discern, completely outside the Cult of the Next Thing. She doesn't even defy it: she ignores it.

Helen has every reason to fear scarcity: never to say enough, never to say thank you. She grew up in Russia during Stalin's purges and engineered famines, and her family, of German origin, suffered terribly. When she was still in her early teens, she and five other girls from her village fled to Germany. It was a harrowing journey—across frozen or muddy fields, slipping through tangles of barbed wire. They left almost everything. On the way, they lost two children from disease. Several times they came close to starving. There are photos of them with stark flesh and sharp bones, eyes defiant and sorrowful and afraid, gathered in a huddle. Their clothes hang loose.

Her family later tried to join her. But the Russians caught up with Helen's parents and siblings and sent them in stinking, crammed cattle cars to Siberia, where her parents died.

Helen remained in Germany. She worked there for a woman who threatened to shoot her if she ever tried to leave. She didn't try. Anyway, Hitler found her useful: he put her to work digging ditches for his war. There is a photo of Helen, rawboned in a plain dirndl, standing with other women beside a pile of raw, wet earth. They hold shovels. Guards are in the background, at the edge of the photo. The women smile. The guards don't.

After the war, Helen came to Canada. She had a cousin in Manitoba, a prosperous Realtor and a church elder, and he and his wife took Helen in as their housemaid. Helen believed the grief was over, now only a memory to scatter under the weight of forgetting and forgiving. She was wrong. Her cousin raped her, repeatedly. She owed her cousin and his wife the money for sponsoring her trip to Canada. She didn't yet speak English. Alone, afraid, she gave in to him. Helen got pregnant. Both the church and her cousin's family banished her and the child.

Helen came west. In time she married and lived modestly. Several years ago, her husband died and left her a small pension. She has every reason to hoard, to hide, to be angry. She has every reason to have banished the words *thank you* and *enough* from her speaking and thinking. And yet those words define her life, shape its inner places and outward forms.

Money, things—they don't give freedom.

One day in church as I led prayer, I asked if there was anyone who would like to thank God for anything. Helen stood up. "Oh, Pastor Mark," she said. "I praise God!"

"Tell us about it, Helen."

"Well, the other day, it was such a beautiful day, I decided to wash my car, and as I'm washing, what do I notice? My insurance expired three days earlier. Well, right away, I walked downtown and bought new insurance. Then, I was telling a friend of mine about it, and she said, 'You're lucky. That happened to me, and the police stopped me. I was fined three hundred dollars.'"

I thought that was the end of her story—praising God that the police didn't catch her. But it wasn't the end of the story.

Helen continued, "God has given me three hundred dollars. That's how I see it. The Lord has done this. So I asked, 'Lord, what am I to do with this three hundred dollars?' He said, 'Give it to the church.' So today, I have three hundred dollars to give to the church, and I'm praising God."

Another time, our church held a business meeting. The big vote that night was whether to hire a youth pastor. Our church finances had not been strong, and many people were saying that we just couldn't afford a youth pastor, even though the need was great.

Helen got up. She is seventy-three years old. She has one daughter—her child from her cousin—who is middle-aged. She has four grandchildren, who live in another city. Helen has two stepdaughters with children. They also live elsewhere. She has no vested interest in youth work in our church.

Helen said, "When I lived in Russia, growing up, I wanted so much to have a piano and to play it. But I could never afford it. When I married, we had a piano, but I never learned to play it. Last month, I decided that I could now afford sixty dollars a month and fulfill my dream since I was a girl. I signed up for piano lessons." She stopped. Her voice was breaking. She continued, slow, soft. "Tonight, I realize that our young people are far more important than my learning how to play the piano. I love young people and want them to know about Jesus. So I am going to quit piano lessons and give that money every month for a youth pastor."

That changed everything. The church voted unanimously to hire a youth pastor. It's what one person can do who, having enough, being continuously thankful, pays no tribute to the Cult of the Next Thing.

GOD VS. THE PIG-GOD

Money, things—they don't give freedom. Freedom, rather, is in the opposite direction, in refusing to love money, to pay Things an honor they don't deserve, to give to the Cult an affection it will never requite. To live, real freedom requires something more than, other than, force of will. Earlier, I spoke about defying Mammon, breaking out of his cult. But that in itself leads nowhere. Once we defy it, then what? If we refuse the lure of the Next Thing, what will we replace it with?

The answer is God. We will live—fully, joyfully—in the presence of God. Consumerism's worst effect is it shunts us away from God's presence. It always ushers us into the wrong place. Is it possible that the God who made the heavens and the earth, who hewed mountains and poured seas, the God who raises the dead, the God who knit you together in your mother's womb, numbered your days, knows your thoughts, knows you by name, and says to you, "Everything I have is yours"—is it possible, I'm asking, that that's not enough? That we won't be happy until our kitchen is renovated, or we've bought a better car, or visited Europe? And then we won't be happy anyway? Is that possible? The Cult of the Next Thing guarantees it.

Is God who he says he is? That is the crux. If God isn't, then "let's eat, drink, and be merry. . . . What's the difference, for tomorrow we die."[85] But if God is God, it is only a cruel form of self-spite to spurn the true God for a lesser god—especially a sloppy, bullying ingrate like Mammon, the pig-god, and his miserable cult.

Joyce Carol Oates wrote a novel a few years ago called *Because It Is Bitter, and Because It Is My Heart*. The title comes from a Stephen Crane poem about a beast who devours his own heart and, when asked why, responds with that line. Oates's novel is about a young black boy and a young white girl in middle America in the 1950s. They fall in love, but of course everything in their world wars against their doing anything about that. Their options are completely shut down. All they can do, all they have freedom for, are acts of self-spite—self-mutilation, self-humiliation, self-recrimination, self-punishment. They resort to it and destroy the promise of their own lives.

The only freedom the Cult of the Next Thing grants us is acts of self-spite. Because it is bitter, and because it is my heart. Mammon has no need to hurt us. Worship him, you devour yourself. The stunning folly of this, the bewildering tragedy, is that we can choose otherwise.

"Stay away from the love of money; be satisfied with what you have. For God has said, 'I will never, never fail you nor forsake you.'"[86]

Is that enough to be thankful for?

PART V

PERIPHERAL VISION

If anybody ever had good reason to fixate on a goal or destination, it was Jesus on the way to the cross. He knew exactly what he had to accomplish and what it would cost him. He also knew that his time on earth was brief, and that he had much to accomplish. How then, did he have time for people like Zacchaeus, an odd little man up in the branches of a sycamore tree . . . or for blind Bartimaeus, crying out from the side of the road passing through Jericho?

For all his great mission, and even though he remained aware of the road he had to travel, Jesus maintained his peripheral vision. He stopped to listen to people and meet their needs, whether it was the woman with the issue of blood who touched the edge of his cloak as he was passing by, or the paralyzed man whose friends interrupted his sermon after dismantling the roof.

It's an important reminder for all of us. No matter how keenly we feel our "call," or no matter how busy we are advancing the kingdom, we need to have eyes for the needy people in our peripheral vision . . . people almost out of our sight, but never out of Christ's.

In this section Gordon MacDonald, Skye Jethani, Mark Labberton, and Donald Sunukjian share insights about balancing life's most pressing demands with an eye for those along our path—who might need a word, a touch, a helping hand, or even just a genuine, from-the-heart smile.

15

MENTORING OTHERS TO SPIRITUAL MATURITY

———— ⊙ ————

Cultivating People of Spiritual Depth Is Top Priority

GORDON MACDONALD

Recently I have been drawn to the word *deep* as a descriptor when I speak of mature Christians. My earliest appreciation for the term came when I read a comment by Richard Foster: "The desperate need today is not for a greater number of intelligent people, or gifted people, but for deep people."[87]

What does it mean to be a deep Christ-follower today when unlimited options, noisy distractions, and a million versions of truth swamp the soul? How is it possible to be a deep person while being swept up in a fifty- or sixty-hour workweek (if you're working), community and school events, shopping, networking, laundering, family-building . . . oh, and staying on top of things at church too? Is deep even thinkable for anyone living outside of a monastery? I'm just asking.

Of course we can't even attempt to answer these questions until we explore what deep means. Here's my working definition: Deep people are those whose lives are organized around Jesus, his character, his call to a serving life, and his death on the cross for their sins. The abilities (or giftedness) of deep people may be quite diverse, but each has the power to influence others to follow Jesus, grow in

Christ-likeness, and live a life of faithful service. They love the world, mix well with people, but are wary of spiritual entrapments. They are known for their wisdom, their compassion for others, and their perseverance in hard times.

HOW IMPORTANT IS DEPTH?

Now, consider this statement: A church's greatest treasure is its deep people. I know recent church emphasis has valued seekers, young people, and people that reflect diversity—all important elements of a healthy church. But absent a core of deep people, a church is in trouble. Deep people do not just happen; they are cultivated. Let's take this thought one step further. Deep people are a treasure greater than a church's preacher; greater than its hottest program; even greater than its worship band. I can hear teeth gnashing.

If the previous paragraph is true, then consider the following:

- A high percentage of a church's deep people should be laypeople, those whose lives are lived in the marketplace, the school, or the community.
- Church leaders should be aware of who their deep people are, just as much as they know where their money is . . . or isn't.
- Church leaders should imagine an approach to ministry that makes the continuous cultivation of deep people (of every age) its highest priority.
- Churches should consider assigning this cultivation effort to their lead pastors, noting it as their top responsibility.

What would it mean for a church to accept these propositions? Well, what if—hang with me here—the first paragraph of the lead pastor's job description were to read: "The first priority of the lead pastor is to serve as the chief (spiritual) development officer of the entire congregation. He or she will be held personally accountable by the church board to train a certain number of men and women each year qualified to offer spiritual leadership inside and beyond the church organization."

Two developments have prompted these thoughts. The first is a growing suspicion that many churches are no longer producing many (if any) truly deep people. Something is not working. The Willow Creek Association self-study, called REVEAL, seems to speak to this when it expresses concern for the paucity of mature Christians to be developed by mere involvement in church programs. I've done my own unscientific, anecdotal study. Wherever I go in North America and in other parts of the world, I ask pastors these questions:

- How many deep people do you know? This often generates a discussion on what deep people look like (see above) and the quiet admission that the number of them is small.
- Any chance we're calling people to an unlivable faith?
- If not, do you think your church is producing deep people? (This, all too frequently, causes a thoughtful silence and an inventory of discipleship programs that mostly seem to work, but only for a short time.)
- Do you personally, as pastor, spend time identifying and mentoring potentially deep people? (This often leads to conversations on how few hours there are in a workweek.)

The answers I get to these questions are occasionally encouraging. But most lead me to conclude that a lot of pastors concentrate on what draws crowds (often preaching) but neglect what cultivates deep people (usually mentoring).

But what if most preaching events rarely produce deep people? What if preaching tends rather to inspire, to inform, to provide practical Christian advice—but little more?

These are important functions. But if the premier challenge in ministry leadership is to develop deep people, as described, for example, in Paul's words, "rooted and built up in him, strengthened in the faith as ... taught, and overflowing with thankfulness,"[88] then we may need to rethink how life-altering ministry is accomplished.

Occasionally, when I talk to pastors about these things, I am reminded that larger churches often have a staff person responsible for "discipleship." This usually means small-group programs. These are often very good people.

But sometimes I push back by saying that, if populating the church with increasing numbers of deep people is a church's highest priority, then that priority cannot be delegated to associate staff. It must be led, and led aggressively, I suggest, by the senior leader. Only then will the congregation get the message that this deep-people-cultivation stuff is really important. In other words, the lead pastor must be first cultivator.

WHAT DID JESUS DO?

One day I asked myself: If Jesus read the classifieds on the *Christianity Today* website and decided to apply for a ministry job, which one would he choose? Lead pastor? Soup kitchen operator? Denominational executive? Custodian? Children's worker?

Apparently most of the hours of Jesus' public ministry were invested in a small number of men and women who, under his mentorship, morphed into deep people and set in motion a movement that continues to this day. No question about it: this mentoring activity was Jesus at his best, his sweet spot.

So, in what capacity did he do it? Like many do it today? Form a circle and fill in the blanks of a Bible-study booklet? Hold a series of Tuesday evening meetings and show videos of inspirational speakers? I don't think so.

Jesus cultivated deep people in the traditional way of the rabbis. So how did rabbis go about reshaping peoples' lives? In a way considerably different than ours.

Like most rabbis of his time, Jesus did preach. But it was a very different sort of preaching. Much of it was dialogical: story-telling, questions and answers, argument. It bore little resemblance to the monologues of today's preachers. If someone interrupted my preaching, as they apparently did in Jesus' time, I'd be horrified.

Strangely enough, much of Jesus' preaching would have earned him low grades in today's preaching courses. I mean, how would you grade a preacher who started with a curious crowd of thousands that dwindled to an audience of twelve, who themselves were hardly paragons of fidelity?

Yet Jesus seemed unconcerned with empty seats. What he does appear to have cared about is what the twelve were going to be and do. I'm left to assume that Jesus the rabbi was less a preacher and more a cultivator-coach to those disciples he'd chosen. What he did with them and how he did it, I call the genius of the rabbinical contract.

I never used to take Jesus' status as a rabbi seriously. With apologies to my Jewish friends, I thought his role as a rabbi was incidental. Then I took a fresh look at the Lord's life and realized that this status as an itinerant rabbi was crucial to understanding his ministry approach. His mission was to redeem and reframe the lives of those who would extend this mission after he was gone. Rabbis, like parents, always had their eyes on the future. Who would perpetuate their teaching?

It's likely that at the age of twelve, Jesus stood out among his peers for his remarkable ability to master the Torah and his aptitude for engaging with people, including those much older than he. Luke says people really liked Jesus.

A speculative question might be raised: Who was Jesus' rabbi when he was young? Who was his teacher?

I've no idea, but don't ignore one special person: his mother. She had to have had a profound influence upon his development. She was clearly one tough and intelligent lady (reread the *Magnificat*). I'm sure that she read the prophet Isaiah to her son every time she had the chance. You can almost hear her saying, "Son, the proud, the powerful, and the rich are not where it's at. Keep your eye out for the poor, the hungry, and the oppressed. Tell them they're loved." And he did.

If the premier challenge in ministry leadership is to develop deep people then we may need to rethink how life-altering ministry is accomplished.

At the age of thirty Jesus left his family trade and hit the road as a rabbi-teacher. Itinerant rabbis moved from town to town and conducted seminar-type meetings with local people who usually welcomed them and hoped for a miracle or a revolution. In another time we might have called what Jesus did barnstorming. Each of these roaming rabbis possessed a somewhat unique interpretation of the Torah, and their collections of teachings were known as their "word" (as in "my word will not pass away") or even their "gospel." It was said that a rabbi "received" his teaching from one who'd gone before him.

Most visible in the life of a rabbi were his students or disciples. They were usually a small, carefully vetted group of younger men who followed the teacher. In some cases, disciples got into this rabbinical relationship because their families negotiated with the rabbi in a way not dissimilar to the way a parent might try to get a son or daughter into a top college or university.

The better connected a family was in the social network, the greater a young man's chances of connecting with a highly-regarded rabbi. Paul reflects this arrangement when he supports his claim to be an authentic Jew. "Under Gamaliel I was thoroughly trained,"[89] he says. Today he might have put it this way: "I got my degree from the College of Gamaliel."

We have several descriptions of how things developed between Jesus and his disciples. When Jesus spent time on the boat with Peter and other fishermen, Peter told him, "Depart from me, for I am a sinful man."[90]

Peter simply could not visualize himself as a disciple. Too much of a past, he may have reasoned; too many character defects; too many other ambitions. He seemed to see no way he could be what Jesus' rabbinical contract would require.

Jesus' response—"from now on you will catch men"[91]—doubtlessly builds off an extensive earlier conversation. In the end Jesus broke through Peter's resistance and drew him away from his trade and into a life of learning and serving.

In telling us this story, the gospel writers seem to assume that we, the readers, are conversant with the drama of the disciple-picking event. They seem to assume we know that this leaving of the nets was no instant decision, but that it had been discussed, proposed, pondered. And now the thinking became actionable. Peter and the others enter the rabbinical contract.

In the times that followed, Peter's rogue opinions and impulsive behaviors appear to vindicate his original opinion of himself. He was no "rock" in those early days, and most of us—had we been the rabbi—would probably have offloaded him at the first opportunity.

Jesus' further choice to call both Matthew (tax collector) and Simon (of the Zealot movement) is stunning when you think about it. The two men could easily have killed each other! Their political positions were as different as those of Bill Maher and Rush Limbaugh.

The twelve Jesus picked were diverse in their personalities, backgrounds, and expectations. Few of us would dare to put these people in the same room together, much less anticipate depth from them.

HOW DO YOU DEEPEN A DISCIPLE?

So how did Jesus deepen these men? Three answers: emulation, information, and examination.

Emulation: The disciples of a rabbi sought to mimic everything about their mentor. What did he think? How did he talk? How did he eat? Disciples desired to be flawless copies of their rabbi. They believed that the rabbi was the incarnation of the Torah, and they, in turn, wished for others to see the example of the rabbi in them. Now we can understand Paul when he says: "I want to know Christ . . . [even] in his death."[92] To know was to be like.

Information: The rabbi might teach in the Temple area, but often rabbis taught away from a classroom and out on the roads, in the fields, in the marketplace, at the lakeshore. Everything in ordinary life became an illustration of the rabbi's teaching; most everything was taught in story form or in riddles and proverbs designed to make a point and challenge the disciple's mind. Rabbis were unafraid to leave conclusions up in the air. Even Jesus tells stories with no obvious application. It's as if he likes to say, "Go figure!"

Examination: Rabbis provided times of testing. Think of Jesus' ministry: the storm, feeding the five thousand, the betrayal in the garden. Times of testing. You can hear Jesus, saying "Where is your faith?" when the storm is quieted. "You give them something to eat," he demands pointing to the crowd. "You're all going to forsake me," he predicts. There were also rebukes: "Get behind me, Satan." And questions: "What were you discussing when I wasn't there?" And assignments: "He sent them to preach the kingdom of God . . ."[93]

When the rabbi decided that the contract had been fulfilled, he discharged his disciples. Again, Jesus: "You're servants no longer; you're friends." "It's best for you that I go away." "You're going to do more than I've done." "Love one another as you've been loved." "Get out into the world and replicate yourselves by teaching what I've taught you."[94]

After saying these things, he left them. His teaching now burned into their heads, his spirit now resident in their hearts. Finally, they were on their way to becoming deep people.

WHAT MIGHT WE LEARN FROM ALL THIS?

You've got to admit it when you review the story: Jesus was an incredible producer of deep people. In three years he made twelve champions. Well, eleven anyway. How do we do what Jesus did?

1. By knowing our "main thing." Is our goal simply to attract a crowd? Or to develop deep people who will carry on Jesus' cause? Developing deep people may not produce instant crowds, but it lays the foundation for a strong and enduring ministry.

2. By not delegating this away. Developing deep people has to be spearheaded by the number one person in the organization. Ask yourself—and this is sort of silly—if Jesus could have accomplished what he came to do if he had turned to John the Baptizer and said, "I'd like to make you my discipleship director. You teach the people what I think is important while I address the larger crowds, cast the vision, raise the money, and network the influencers in the Temple."

3. By helping our churches see that the continuous development of

deep people is among the church's most serious investments, and that pastors are held accountable for their work in pursuing this mandate.

4. By following the strategy of emulation, information, and examination. Admittedly, this takes time, and it probably means that a lead pastor might have to say to the church board, "I'm going to invest 20 percent of my time in twelve to fifteen people each year, and you're going to have to support me when the congregation begins to ask why I'm not around for a lot of program events."

The strategy of the rabbinical contract probably requires time away from church property, being out of the view of the larger congregation. The pastor's home might be a good place to start. The would-be disciples' workplaces could be another. Any venue where growth can be taught, illustrated, and tested is a useful place.

A fifth thought. Rabbis are not necessarily nice guys. They constantly raise the bar on their disciples. They are not reluctant to open up their own lives; they know how to poke into the inner space of their disciples; they know how to bring out the best in others. Cultivating deep people is serious business.

Paul is thinking about the rabbinical contract when he writes to Timothy, "What I've taught you . . . teach others . . . who will teach others."[95] Do it by being an example, Paul says, "in speech [what and how you say things], in conduct [the way you live], in love [your quality of relationships], in faith [how you trust God], and in purity [your moral choices]."[96] That's all rabbinical talk. "Command, rebuke, exhort?" Also rabbinical. In short: Timothy's assignment was to grow deep people.

Here's a final thought. We're developing disciples of Jesus, not of ourselves. The rabbi's deep people are not his. Disciples are not to be owned, controlled, or misused. They belong to Jesus, and he is free to guide them toward life and leadership in the church but also, possibly, beyond it. The church's greatest treasure—these deep people—must be shared, exported, sent out.

When Jesus prayed before his arrest in the garden, what did he pray for? He prayed for "those whom you gave me." Hear him: "I have revealed you to them . . . I have given them your word . . . they need your protection . . . they need to be sanctified . . . I've sent them out."[97]

He prayed not for the crowds he'd preached to, but for the disciples he'd cultivated.

I have known a "rabbi" or two in my life who guided me through the process of emulation, instruction, and examination. Sometimes they were tough, sometimes tender. They believed in the present and future me. They saw what I might become and endeavored to deepen me. They are all gone now. I miss them greatly. But I have their "word," and I'm committed to handing their gospel on to others.

16

YIELD THE RIGHT-OF-WAY

———— ◉ ————

Seeing the World As Jesus Sees It

SKYE JETHANI

In Matthew chapter 5, beginning with verse 38, Jesus says: "You have heard that it was said, 'Eye for eye, and tooth for tooth.' But I tell you, Do not resist an evil person. If someone strikes you on the right cheek, turn to him the other also. And if someone wants to sue you and take your tunic, let him have your cloak as well. If someone forces you to go one mile, go with him two miles. Give to the one who asks you, and do not turn away from the one who wants to borrow from you" (NIV).

Now, if you were an African American living in the south in the 1950s, how would you hear this? If you were a Jew living in Europe in the late 1930s, how do you hear this? If you're a victim of injustice, bigotry, or persecution, how do you hear this? The problem we have with Jesus' teaching, both here and throughout the Sermon on the Mount, is that a lot of it does not fit with our experiences in this world.

Many of us experience hatred and violence and injustice and persecution, and then we come to the words of Jesus and he says: Turn the other cheek? Do good to those who mean to harm you? Give your shirt when they've already stolen your coat? It doesn't make sense. Even if you've grown up your whole life in the church, even if you've been taught these verses, even if you have them memorized, the fact is when you come up against some kind of evil or danger or threat, a lot of times these words get thrown out the window. They don't make sense when we're in that moment.

A story from Eugene Peterson about a schoolboy experience illustrates the point. He says:

> I grew up in a Christian home with good parents. I was told the story of Jesus and instructed in the Jesus way. . . .
>
> And then I went off to school and discovered what the Gospel of John named 'the world' . . . This knowledge entered my life in the person of Garrison Johns, the school bully. . . .
>
> About the third day [in school], Garrison discovered me and took me on as his project for the year. . . . I had been taught in Sunday school not to fight. . . . I had [memorized] "Bless those who persecute you" and "Turn the other cheek." . . . Most afternoons after school [Garrison] would catch me and beat me up. . . .
>
> I tried to find alternate ways home by making detours through alleys, but he stalked me and always found me.
>
> And then something unexpected happened. I was with my neighborhood friends on this day, seven or eight of them, when Garrison caught up with us and started in on me, jabbing and taunting, working himself up to the main event.
>
> That's when it happened. Totally uncalculated. Totally out of character. Something snapped within me. For just a moment the Bible verses disappeared from my consciousness and I grabbed Garrison. To my surprise, and his, I real-

ized that I was stronger than he was. I wrestled him to the ground, sat on his chest, and pinned his arms to the ground with my knees. I couldn't believe it—he was helpless. . . . At my mercy. It was too good to be true. I hit him in the face with my fists. It felt good, and I hit him again—blood spurted from his nose, a lovely crimson on the snow. By this time all the other children were cheering, egging me on. "Black his eyes!" "Bust his teeth!" A torrent of biblical invective poured from them. . . .

I said to Garrison, "Say 'Uncle.'" He wouldn't say it. I hit him again. More blood, more cheering. . . . And then my Christian training reasserted itself. I said, "Say 'I believe in Jesus Christ as my Lord and Savior.'" . . .

And he said it. Garrison Johns was my first Christian convert.[98]

Here's the problem with the Sermon on the Mount, particularly these words of Jesus about vengeance. We can learn them, we can study them, we can memorize them—but when we come face to face with the Garrison Johnses of this world, the Bible verses disappear and we face the reality of a dangerous, threatening, scary world in which justice is hard to come by, goodness is often hidden under the shadow of evil, and hatred seems stronger than love. The problem with Jesus' teaching in the Sermon on the Mount is that it just doesn't fit with our experience of the world.

So we have two options: either we dismiss Jesus as absurd, or we need to reevaluate our understanding of this world. These two options are mutually exclusive; they can't both be right. One of them has to give. That's the core tension we must come to terms with.

JESUS CONFIRMS THAT THE LAW DOESN'T REHABILITATE OUR HEARTS

In order to understand what Jesus is getting at here, we need to do a little background work. In Matthew 5:38, he says, "You have heard it said, 'Eye for eye, and tooth for tooth.'" He's quoting the Old Testament, the Torah. What we often fail to recognize is that at the time God gave this law to Moses, it was actually quite revolutionary. You see, there was a major problem in the ancient world (and in a lot of our world today) with vengeance escalating out of control. Consider it this way: you insult me, I hit you; you hit me, I cut you; you cut me, I shoot you; you shoot me, I shoot your whole family. It's the plot of every gangster movie that's ever been made.

So God steps in and gives his people a command that is supposed to put a check on how far vengeance is allowed to go. He tells them, "An eye for an eye, a tooth for a tooth," meaning the punishment should not exceed the offense. You are not justified in retaliating worse against somebody for what he or she did to you. He's putting a boundary, a check, a guardrail around how far vengeance can go, and his desire was to preserve his people—to protect them from this escalation of vengeance.

This is important because we often come to the Sermon on the Mount, particularly to these verses about vengeance, and we think that Jesus is saying that the Old Testament law is bad. I don't believe that's what he's saying. In fact, earlier he said, "I didn't come to abolish the law, I came to fulfill it."[99] He's not saying that "eye for an eye, tooth for a tooth" is wrong or bad or evil or unjust. He recognizes that it's a good command given by God to put barriers, parameters, or guardrails around how far vengeance is allowed to go for the preservation of his people. But just because a law is good doesn't mean it's best. And that's how we have to understand what Jesus is saying here.

Not long ago, I rented the 1962 film, *The Birdman of Alcatraz* which is loosely based on a true story. Burt Lancaster plays a convicted murderer named Robert Stroud, who is sentenced to a life term in Alcatraz. The core tension of the film is between Stroud, the convict, and the warden, Harvey Shumaker. The two men spend three decades together in the prison system, and toward the end of the film they get into a really tense but interesting conversation about the nature of real rehabilitation. One section of that conversation illustrates something important about law. Stroud, the convict, says this to the warden:

> I wonder if you even know what rehabilitation means. The *Unabridged Webster's International Dictionary* says it comes from the Latin root *habilitas*, meaning to invest again with dignity. Do you consider that part of your job, Harvey? To give a man back the dignity he once had? Your only interest is in how he behaves. You want your prisoners to dance out of the gates like puppets on a string with rubber stamp values impressed by you, with your sense of conformity, your sense of behavior, even your sense of morality. And that's why you're a failure, Harvey. Because once they're on the outside, they're still lost. Just going through the motions of living. And underneath there is a deep, deep hatred. So the first chance they get to attack society, they do it. And the result, more than half of them come back to prison.

Stroud's critique of the prison system helps us understand the limitations of law in general. Laws may be good, laws may be just. Laws may give us a sense of what's right and wrong, a sense of morality. Laws can put barriers, hedges, gates around how far evil is allowed to go. But what law cannot do is truly rehabilitate us. It cannot restore to us the dignity that God wants us to have as the creatures made in his image. What law cannot do is truly take the evil, the anger, the hatred out of our hearts.

Sometimes when we read these verses in the Sermon on the Mount, we make the mistake of believing that Jesus is setting up a more stringent law. But that's not what he is doing. He's not giving us another law. Because law cannot truly rehabilitate. Jesus isn't giving us more rules to follow. What he is doing is illustrating the kind of behavior one will exhibit when the law truly resides in his or her heart. He's illustrating what a person looks like who has been truly rehabilitated by God and is living fully immersed in his kingdom.

Here's another way of putting it: Jesus is not saying that you now have to walk the second mile, that you have to turn the other cheek, and that you have to give up your tunic and your coat. He is not saying you have to do these things. What he is saying is that when you are set free from anger and hatred and evil, when vengeance itself has no root in your heart, when you have been completely rehabilitated, these are the kinds of things you want to do. You will love others so much that you want what is truly good for them. You want to walk the second mile, you want to turn the other cheek, you want to give to those who ask of you. Jesus is not laying out another law for us to obey. He's illustrating for us what a truly rehabilitated heart looks like.

JESUS' WORDS POINT TO A GOD-BATHED WORLD.

Now, you might be thinking: Okay, got it. It's not another law, it's a rehabilitated heart, it's transformation on the inside, it's being set free—all that. Great, Skye, but it still doesn't help. Because how on earth do you become that kind of person? You're facing a Garrison

Johns in your life. You're facing hatred, persecution, evil, injustice. How do you keep the fists from flying? How does this transformation actually take root?

I'll begin my answer to that question with a story. In 1956, Martin Luther King, Jr., was a young twenty-something Baptist preacher in Montgomery, Alabama. Through some odd circumstances, he found himself as the leader of the bus boycott that began when Rosa Parks refused to give up her seat on a bus. And as the boycott progressed, King started hearing rumors that the white authorities in Montgomery wanted to get rid of him. In Montgomery, Alabama, in 1956, if you were a black man and someone wanted to get rid of you, you knew what that meant.

It came to a head on the night of January 27th. King was asleep in his small home with his young wife and their two-month-old baby girl when he was awakened by a phone call. I won't quote exactly what the caller said—that would be very inappropriate. But the essence of it was that if King was not out of town in three days, they were going to kill him, and they were going to bomb his house. He hung up the phone, but he was so bothered, so disturbed by this that he couldn't go back to bed. So he poured himself a cup of coffee, sat down at his kitchen table, thought about his wife in the bedroom and his baby girl in her crib, sleeping peacefully. To use his language, he was paralyzed by fear.

Few of us have been in circumstances exactly like King faced that night. But I think many of us have probably had that all-too-common human experience of being paralyzed by fear. Is my child okay? Is the diagnosis bad? Am I losing my job? Is my draft number up? The scenarios go on and on. When we feel threatened by an outside force, we turn inward, we become paralyzed. You may have been there. Contracted inward.

That's where Martin Luther King, Jr. was that night over his cup of coffee at his kitchen table. And then something unexpected happened that changed the course of King's life, and a case can be made that it changed the course of American history. As he was sitting there with his face in his hands over his cup of coffee, confessing his fears and his anxieties to God, King said that he felt a stirring in his soul that he'd never felt before. And then he heard a voice—not an audible voice but an inner voice. And this is how King related what the voice said to him: "'Stand up for righteousness, stand up for justice, stand up for truth. And lo, I will be with you, even until the end of the world.' . . . I heard the voice of Jesus . . . He promised never to leave me, never to leave me alone. No, never alone."[100]

In that moment, in the middle of that night, in that hour when darkness reigned, King had a supernatural encounter with the living presence of God. What radically changed Martin Luther King was an inexplicable sense that God was with him, that God had drawn near to him. It changed his life. It changed his outlook. It changed his mission. It changed his perspective. And this, I believe, is the key to understanding Jesus' words about vengeance in Matthew chapter 5. In fact, I would argue that it's the key to understanding the Sermon on the Mount in general. If we don't get this, the rest of it doesn't make sense.

Let's go back to the beginning of the Sermon and look at the Beatitudes in the first part of Matthew 5.

The Beatitudes list the various categories of people who are really blessed. Jesus begins by saying, "Blessed are the poor in spirit." In *The Divine Conspiracy*, Dallas Willard translates it, "Blessed are the spiritual zeros." The people who have no credibility spiritually whatsoever; they are blessed. "Blessed are those who mourn." Blessed are those who cry. Blessed are those who are sad, who are afraid.

Blessed are those who are awake at two in the morning over a cup of coffee, paralyzed by fear. "Blessed are the persecuted." When you are marginalized and hated and set apart, blessed are you. What Jesus is saying, the overwhelming message he has at the beginning of the Sermon on the Mount, is that God is with you. In other words, God is on your side.

This confidence that God is on your side is vitally important because if you truly believe that—and I don't mean just intellectually, but you have come to experience the reality of God with you—it changes the way you see the world.

I like the way Dallas Willard put it. He said that we live in a God-bathed world. Once you come to believe that, he continued, then the only conclusion you can draw is that this world is a perfectly safe place in which to live. The first time I read that I thought Willard was nuts, because I had experienced enough troubles in my life to contradict him: this world is not safe. But think about it. From a cosmic, eternal viewpoint, his logic is sound. If this is a God-with-you world, if this is a God-with-us universe, what do we have to be afraid of? It truly is a perfectly safe place in which to live.

Our perception of the world is that it's a place where justice is hard to come by. Our perception of the world is that it's a place where goodness is always marred by the shadow of evil. Our perception of the world is that life itself is in short supply and must be defended and fought for. But what if we're wrong? What if this really is a God-with-us universe, a God-bathed world? Because if it is, to use the words of the apostle Paul, "If God is for us, who can be against us?"[101]

If this is a God-with-us world, then we don't have to worry that injustice is going to have the last word, because God promises that all things will be made right. Justice will have the last word. If this is a God-bathed world, then goodness is not forever under the shadow of evil, but goodness is expanding and breaking forth with the expansion of his kingdom. And if this is a God-with-us world, life is not in short supply; life is in abundance, and our lives will never end, but are hidden with God in Christ. If this is a God-with-us world, I don't have to be afraid. I don't have to contract inward in self-defense. If this is a God-with-us world, I don't have to hit the person who hit me. I don't have to worry about giving my shirt as well as my coat. In fact, in a God-with-us world, I am so set free from anger, from hatred, from fear that maybe I can actually love the person who means to harm me.

WHAT KIND OF WORLD DO YOU SEE?

Here's the core problem we have with the Sermon on the Mount: it isn't that Jesus' teachings are absurd; it's that we don't see the world that Jesus sees. We see a world of injustice and anger and hatred and violence—a world where everything good is in short supply and life itself is fragile. But Jesus saw a world in which his father was in control, in which justice was guaranteed, in which goodness was breaking forth, and in which life itself is without end. And if you see that world through the lens of the gospel, then what Jesus tells us to do and how he informs us to live makes perfect sense.

So the issue here is not whether or not we resist evil. We are called to be agents of righteousness and justice in this world. The question is, why do we pursue that righteousness and justice? Jesus forbids us from pursuing it out of anger, hatred, or vengeance. We pursue righteousness and justice and goodness because we love God and we love others, even the perpetrators of these evils. So I hope you will not walk away thinking the principle of turning the other cheek means you just have to tolerate everything that happens to you. It means that in everything, we seek what is good for the other, not ourselves.

Just four days after Martin Luther King's coffee-cup conversion, his new vision of the world was put to the test. Four days after this sleepless night at home, he was speaking at a rally for the bus boycott when, around nine o'clock at night, a young man ran into the service and announced that Martin Luther King's house had just been bombed—the house where his wife and two-month-old daughter were staying. King ran out of the rally, ran down the street, and found his home still on fire. The police were there, the fire officials were there, and a large, angry mob of black citizens from Montgomery, Alabama, were around the house with guns and rifles and baseball bats, ready to riot because of this attack on their leader's home.

Once King found that his wife and daughter were safe, he got on the porch of his home that had just been firebombed by the Klan. He stood on that burning porch and he looked out on this angry crowd of black citizens ready to riot, and King preached a sermon. Listen to what he said to them: " Jesus still cries out . . .: 'Love your enemies; bless them that curse you; pray for them that despitefully use you.' This is what we must live by. We must meet hate with love. . . . This movement will not stop, because God is with the movement. Go home with this glowing faith and this radiant assurance."[102]

This is what I love about King. He was first and foremost a preacher. His house is on fire and he thinks, *This is a sermon illustration.* "Go home with this glowing faith and this radiant assurance." Can you just hear him saying that with a night sky ablaze with the fire from his own home? King related that the crowd dispersed and a policeman later told him that "a race riot would probably have broken out" over the smallest incident that night. "This well could have been the darkest night in Montgomery's history," King reflected. "But something happened to avert it: the spirit of God was in our hearts; and a night that seemed destined to end in unleashed chaos came to a close in a majestic group demonstration of nonviolence."[103] How do you explain that shift from a posture of inward fear and contraction to one of outward courage and love? No law can do that; only the presence of God himself does that.

God with us.

Toward the end of the *Birdman of Alcatraz*, Robert Stroud is released from prison (which actually does not happen in real life, but artistic license enabled them to let him out in the movie). He takes the boat from Alcatraz to San Francisco. He gets off the boat, and there's a reporter waiting for him. The reporter asks, "What are you going to do now that you're out of prison?" And Stroud gives a very bizarre answer. He says, "I don't know. Maybe I'll go measure the clouds." What a strange response! But it's rather poetic if you consider the circumstances. He had been in prison for almost forty years— something symbolic of that contraction, that fearful, law-based conformity. And now he is set free. And the imagery of going from a prison cell to measuring the clouds is kind of beautiful.

For me, that imagery also illustrates the absurdity of the Christian life. If we live the way Jesus lived, if we do the things that Jesus says to do in the Sermon on the Mount, people are going to think we are completely out of our minds. We are going to appear as silly as some guy on a ladder holding up a ruler trying to measure the clouds. Think about it. Turn the other cheek; go the second mile. The reason why we look so crazy as Christians is because we see a world that the rest don't see. We see a God-bathed world in which we are perfectly safe. So safe, so set free from fear that we can even love our enemies without thought of the consequence.

Before I wrap up, I want to make sure you've picked up what I've intended and not what I haven't. No doubt many of you reading this have suffered experiences of unbelievable evil and injustice. Some of you are struggling deeply, asking, how do I begin to show goodness and kindness even to those who would harm me, or who have harmed me? The last thing in the world I want is for you to feel burdened, thinking that you just have to try harder. Remember, Jesus is not giving us a new law. His intention is not to burden us with a heavier, more stringent interpretation of the Old Testament Torah.

Because the law doesn't rehabilitate.

The question you should be asking yourself is not, "How could I try harder to love people?" The question you should be asking is, "What kind of world do I see?" Do you see a world of evil and danger and threats and Garrison Johns—a world in which your life is in constant peril, in which you must contract inward even to the point of paralysis? Or do you see a God-bathed world, a God-with-you world, a world of justice and goodness and life without end?

If you're still caught in the vision of the world that we receive from all around us— a vision of fear and threat and danger—don't feel guilty about that. I encourage you to do what Martin Luther King did: Confess your fears to God, acknowledge the vengeance and the hate that is still in your heart. Be honest with him, reveal it. And then invite him to come near. Invite the Spirit of God to inexplicably, unbelievably, supernaturally draw near to you so that you might experience the reality that he is with you always, even to the very end of the world.

And as you experience that truth more and more in your life, you might just find that you are being set free from your fear, that you're not contracted as much, that you're expanding in courage and grace—maybe even to the point of loving those who have been unlovable to you. You might just come to be an agent of justice and goodness and life in this world rather than selfishly hoarding it to yourself. You might live a life so absurd, so ridiculous that it seems like you're standing on a ladder holding up a ruler, and that's okay. We are not to be understood in this world, because we are the people of Christ. But first we must learn to live in this world with him so that we can learn to live like him.

17

THE FIRST RULE OF THE ROAD: LOVE

———— ⊙ ————

The Good News Is Greater Than We Make It Out to Be

MARK LABBERTON

Why does the gospel look to so many like a bowl of lima beans? For those who find the grace and truth of Jesus Christ convincing and compelling, such a question may seem absurd, if not blasphemous. But compared to the spiciness of the cultural concoctions that swirl around us in our globalized world, Jesus can seem like bland fare. Many have the impression that the gospel is small, smooth, and tasteless. They have a culturally conditioned disdain for any homogeneous answer to a heterogeneous world. And they have seen too little evidence to the contrary.

How could it be, some believers might balk, that "the hope of the world," the One given "the name above every name," could ever seem bland? Well, because often the church is bland. Pale. Gullible. Pasty. Just there. The fruit of this vine appears to be lima beans. If bland is the flavor of the church, then it is presumed to be the flavor of the One the church calls Lord.

This anemic image of Jesus has many adherents, both in and outside the church. Their innocuous Jesus is the result of social, political, economic, and spiritual accommodation. Who needs more from Jesus than some simple stories of a loving example? To go further would be zealous, and to be religiously zealous is definitely not a current cultural ideal. Those in the church who stand out are often seen as intolerant and intolerable. Better the disdainfully bland than the dangerously zealous.

It's a misstep, some would say, to take Jesus—his example and his teaching—too seriously. To do so is to get too close to all those details that hound religious specialists, breed religious acrimony, and cause war. Jesus from ten thousand feet away is close enough. The Google Earth view of Jesus identifies only the most prominent features of his life and teachings, bringing nothing too close and taking nothing too seriously. Such a Jesus may be vaguely interesting, but he is consigned to blandness and faint praise.

Jesus Christ, the Lord of Creation, Redemption, and Fulfillment, calls the church the salt and light of the world. Jesus seems to have had in mind a community engaged in vigorous, self-sacrificing mission that goes to great lengths to enact costly love, that inconveniences itself regularly to seek justice for the oppressed, that creatively serves the forgotten, all to portray that the kingdom of God is at hand.

Depending on where we look in the world, however, that church seems to have gone missing.

Rather than seek the God who spoke from the burning bush, we have decided the real drama is found in debating whether to podcast our services. Rather than encounter the God who sees idolatry as a pervasive, life-threatening temptation, we decorate Pottery Barn lives with our tasteful collections of favored godlings. Rather than follow the God who burns for justice for the needy, we are more likely to ask the Lord to give us our own fair share. A bland God for a bland church, with a mission that is at best innocuous and quaint—in a tumultuous world.

Is it hard to explain why many look at the church and see a bowl of lima beans? Where is the evidence that the reality is otherwise, that the gospel really matters?

THE HOMOGENEOUS GOSPEL

Others take a different point of view, and think the gospel is too small. Its claims in a multicultural, multi-religious world are just too particular. Christian orthodoxy's affirmation—that through a promise to one people fulfilled through one man, the one true God reconciled the world to himself—seems by definition too small because it is just too homogenizing a solution. Too small to be worthy of the Creator of the universe, and too "one-size-fits-all" to be the Good News for our enormously varied world.

Postmoderns are keenly aware that we live in a vastly heterogeneous world—of cultures within cultures, of languages within languages, of religions within religions. They are likely to find it extremely counterintuitive that a single religion or deity could possibly reflect reality. In this world of variety, uniform solutions in politics, economics, and culture are unappealing, undesirable, and unworkable. How can that be any less so when it comes to matters of religion and spirituality?

From a theological point of view, they might go on, how could such particularity be consistent with the Bible's own depiction of God's expansive character and nature? Would such a god deserve to be called God, if it all boils down to one way or no way? How could a God who reputedly created a world with three hundred kinds of hummingbirds be the same God who requires religious conformity?

Isn't this alleged particularity of God scandalously less nuanced than the enormously varied created order he is supposed to have made? Further, if those reputedly bearing the image of this God are called to one religious vision, doesn't that diminish their created diversity, homogenizing what God has made varied? If there are over five hundred varieties of bananas, how could God offer the world one bowl of lima beans?

THE EVIDENCE OF LOVE

The love of Jesus Christ, through whom God is reconciling the whole world to himself, is no lima bean. And the only adequate answer to these objections will require us to consider again that very thing Jesus says is central to God's kingdom, the most life-enlarging and non-homogenizing reality: love.

The primary evidence that the gospel is no lima bean is meant to be the compelling, sacrificial love and justice vividly lived and humbly witnessed to by Christ's body. "By this all men will know that you are my disciples, if you love one another."[104] Such love is meant, at the very least, to make our lives more truth-bearing, more soul-enlarging, more justice-evidencing. To give ourselves in love is to devote ourselves to "the more important matters of the law: justice, mercy and faithfulness," rather than fiddling with our "mint, dill and cumin."[105]

Of course, this does not mean our gospel will be more immediately attractive or more easily accepted. A gospel whose evidence is this kind of love may still be accused of being small, but it will be small like the pearl of great price, not like some cheap imitation.

We have to give up the small gospel that simply confirms what C. S. Lewis called "our congenital preference for safe investments and limited liabilities."[106] The freedom of grace grants us many gifts, including that there is "therefore now no condemnation for those who are in Christ Jesus."[107] This assurance of grace is meant to set us on the road of faithful discipleship, not just to assure us of grace at the finish line.

Such freedom enables Christ's disciples to love because we have first been loved.[108] The grace that settles our account with God is meant to set us free from self-interest for the sake of loving others with abandon.

The apparent smallness of our gospel is directly related to the smallness of the church's love. When prominent Christian voices call for protests and boycotts over things like our freedom to say "Merry Christmas," the gospel seems very small indeed. If, by contrast, such voices called the church in America to give away its Christmas billions to the poor and needy around the world—as an act of incarnational love—that would leave a very different impression of the faith we profess, and offer a far greater hope for a love-hungry world.

It would be a new day for our testimony to the immensity and scope of the gospel if we lived out persevering, sacrificial love for people near and far, especially for those without power, money, education, food, sanitation, safety, and faith. If this counterintuitive, servant love moved us out of our middle-class enclaves, drew the poor to be included in our family values, brought us to worry more about the need for consumption of those who have nothing than the consumptive fantasies of those who have too much, the gospel would be more nearly the life-enlarging gift it is.

THE SIZE OF LOVE

Love is central in responding to the charge of particularity as well. What do we say to those who claim our gospel of one way, one truth, and one life is too small? The biblical argument is that God's very particular actions are precisely what give us the greatest access to the universal scope of God's heart and purposes. When God's work is most intensive, the implications are the most extensive: "God so loved the world that he gave his only begotten Son."[109] God in Jesus Christ does the most particular thing for the most universal end.

We must make the case that the particularity of love is like the proper use of a telescope: through the small end of the telescope (i.e., God was in Christ), we are given a glimpse into the cosmic heart of God (i.e., God is love). Through the particularity of the small lens, we are given a way to see the larger reality. The specificity of the gospel is the way God leads us to see what is universal.

This is obvious in ordinary experience. We come to know the meaning of love by loving and being loved by particular people in particular places and times. We don't come to know love first as a broad category and then as a particular instance. Rather, only if we are loved in particular do we gradually come to love more broadly. The absence of the particular leads most likely to the absence of the general ability.

It is true that being loved in particular does not necessarily lead us to love more widely. Still, the more noteworthy this absence of love in people's lives, the more we suspect a deficit of an experience of being loved. And that is precisely what millions of unchurched people suspect about Christians, and therefore about the gospel we proclaim: without more-evident fruit of self-sacrificing love, not least when we are affirming the God of love, the more our claim of particularity seems corrupt, bankrupt, or worse.

The particularity of our sun is not a problem, because it shines on the just and on the unjust. So does God's particular love in Christ. The church cannot afford to give the impression that the particularity of the gospel only shines on us. If we love as we have been loved, the immensity and scope of God's intimate and cosmic gospel in Jesus Christ will be more evidently the salt and light of the world. We will be far more like Jesus described us—tangy and tangible Good News. And that is no lima bean gospel.

18

SEE WITH THE EYES OF A DOCTOR

———— ◉ ————

Why You Should Move into Your Neighbor's World

DONALD SUNUKJIAN

Let's suppose that on your way to work each morning, you usually stop at a Starbucks. You tend to get to the store at the same time each morning, and you usually see a young girl who gets there about the same time you do. On many mornings you find yourselves standing next to each other in line. In fact, you both order the same thing—double espresso with skim milk.

She seems to be into the Goth culture—black hair, black clothes, knee-high jackboots, black fingernails, black lipstick, piercings in the nose, lips, ears, and eyebrows, and scattered tattoos. She usually has a backpack that she has to take off to get her money, and sometimes it seems hard for her to hold the backpack, get the money, and pay for the coffee all at the same time.

She doesn't make too much eye contact with others. You wonder whether you should strike up a conversation with her—maybe offer to hold her backpack while she pays. You're not sure what to do with the whole Goth bit, and you don't know whether she'd give you a dark look and not say anything.

Should you try to be friendly? Maybe find out what brings you both to the same Starbucks each morning? See if she ever tries any of the other specialty coffees? Move toward greeting her each morning? Learn about other parts of her life? Yes! By all means! Move into her world. Make a comment one day about how the barista probably already knows both of your orders as soon as you walk in the door. Offer to hold her backpack while she pays. A couple of days later, tell her your name and ask for hers. If she misses a few days, tell her you hope she wasn't sick the next time you see her.

Why move into her world? Because with the eyes of a doctor, you see a hurt that God can heal. You see an anger and alienation. Maybe it's because of sexual abuse from a stepfather, a brother, or an old boyfriend. But you see the heaviness, the sadness. With the eyes of a doctor, you see a hurt that God can heal.

There's a man at work that all the employees shake their heads at. He's been divorced a couple of times, and both of his ex-wives are suing him for past child support. He's a deadbeat dad—way behind on his support, sending them just a little bit, every so often. He's been living with another woman and her small child, but a couple of weeks ago, he slapped her around pretty hard. She called the cops, he spent a couple nights in jail, she kicked him out, and now he has a restraining order against him. He's currently living in one of the cheap motels that rents by the month.

Every day at lunch, he goes out by himself to get a hamburger or a burrito, always coming back with mustard or chili on his shirt. Nobody talks very much to him, because he's too quick to complain about how everybody's taking advantage of him, everybody's pushing his buttons, everybody's squeezing him dry. Who wants to listen to that?

You've often wondered about being nice and offering to go to lunch with him. You like the same fast food he does—Burger King and Taco Bell and Subway. And you know Subway has a sale going on—three foot-long sandwiches for ten dollars. You couldn't possibly eat that much, but it seems like a shame not to take advantage of such a bargain.

Should you invite him along one day? Yes! By all means! Move into his world. Go to lunch with him. When you get to Subway and you both sit down with your sandwiches and chips and drinks, ask him if he's watched any of the baseball playoffs. Who's he rooting for in the World Series? Mention that it's been just about the worst umpiring you've ever seen.

Why move into his world? Because with the eyes of a doctor, you see a hurt that God can heal. You see a bitterness at life, failing at relationships, blaming others instead of knowing how to change himself. You sense his fear of the future—no money, a criminal record on the books—and his desperation over being all alone in the world. With the eyes of a doctor, you see a hurt that God can heal.

Your company has a co-ed softball team that competes in the city league, and they're looking for a couple of extra players. You like softball. You like the feel of connecting on a pitch, running down a fly ball, making a clothesline throw on one hop to home plate to nail a runner trying to score. The first game is next Tuesday, and they're pushing you to join them.

But you're not sure. You like softball, but you don't know about playing with the people in the office. You went to a company picnic a couple of months ago, where there was a pickup softball game, and some of the guys were drinking a lot of beer, getting pretty raunchy in their comments about some of the women on the other team. Some of the wives of your coworkers were loudmouthed, and they flirted with other husbands. The parents yelled mean things at their children but did nothing to control them. And in the parking lot, one of the married men from the office who had come to the picnic by himself was behind his pickup truck going at it pretty heavy with one of the single moms. Do you want to deal with all that every week?

Should you join the team? Yes! By all means! Move into their world. Get to the park, shag those balls, and run those bases. Bring some Cokes to put in with their beers. When one of the women on the other team lines it into a gap between center and left for a stand-up double, instead of questioning her sexual preference, shout out, "Great hit! Did you play in college?" Buy a cheap glove for the single mom's kid, ask if he wants to be bat boy, have him sit beside you on the bench, and teach him the strategies of the game.

Why move into their world? Because with the eyes of a doctor, you see their hurts that God can heal. You see that the machismo and the raunchiness merely disguise insecurity and failure. You see marriages where there's no love and children that don't have the security of boundaries. You see the single mom's loneliness and vulnerability that puts her at risk of being deeply hurt. With the eyes of a doctor, you see the hurts that God can heal.

THE EYES OF A JUDGE OR THE EYES OF A DOCTOR

In life we can have the eyes of a judge or we can have the eyes of a doctor. The eyes of a judge see a Goth girl, a deadbeat dad, and a foul-mouthed team, and leave us thinking, *Why have anything to do with them?* The eyes of a doctor see the hurts that God can heal.

Do we shun the disreputable—those whose lifestyle is question-able? Do we shut ourselves off from them and have nothing to do with their world? Do we leave them to their anger and despair, their ignorance, their loneliness, their vulnerability? Or do we move into their world—talk with them, laugh with them, eat with them, play with them, be their friend. Do we look at them with the eyes of a judge, seeing choices that God should punish, or do we look at them with the eyes of a doctor, seeing hurts that God can heal?

These are the kinds of questions Mark 2:13–14 forces us to ask. In our passage, we see Jesus moving into the world of someone considered disreputable—someone whose lifestyle was questionable to other people. The man's name is Levi. He's a tax collector. But Jesus invites this disreputable man to be part of his group.

Through his example Jesus is saying to us, "Move into their world as I do, with the eyes of a doctor, seeing the hurts that God can heal."

Let's look a little deeper at the story. After teaching a crowd of people, Jesus is walking along and sees Levi, son of Alphaeus, sitting at the tax collector's booth. "Follow me," Jesus tells him, and Levi gets up and follows him.

Jesus has just come out of the city of Capernaum, which is on the northern shore of the Sea of Galilee. This means that this particular toll station was the one that intercepts all traffic and commerce coming across the border into King Herod's territory. A lot of traffic came that way, because this was the road that connected to Rome in one direction and Egypt in another direction. Levi's job was to collect the tolls—so much per wagon cart, so much per mule—and the import taxes of anyone transporting goods—so much for grain, so much for garments, so much for fish. There would have been a couple of other guys working the tax station with Levi and a couple of soldiers standing by to make sure everybody cooperated.

The taxation process in the New Testament world was oppressive. There were no posted toll costs or tax rates. If you were a merchant, and you rolled into the station with your goods, you had no clue what it was going to cost you to pass through. Levi just came out, counted your carts, poked around in your sacks, checked out all your goods, and then told you how much you had to pay. And you can bet that like all tax collectors in Rome, he was setting the cost high enough so he could send the right amount to King Herod, while also lining his pockets with a little extra cash. Because of the corruption, if you were a merchant, you were at his mercy. After all, the soldiers were there to enforce whatever he said—and he was probably giving them some money on the side to help him out.

All this to say, all the merchants of Jesus' day hated Levi. You can be certain that all the townspeople knew that he was a cheat—no better than a common thief. Nobody wanted anything to do with him. Tax collectors like Levi were so disreputable, so notorious for their dishonesty that they weren't allowed to be witnesses in a court. You just couldn't trust their testimony. It's safe to say that Levi didn't get asked to speak at too many career days at the local elementary school.

And this is why it was so surprising when Jesus came along and moved into Levi's world—even inviting him to be one of his disciples! Jesus had been in the area long enough for Levi to know who he was. Levi had probably heard Jesus teach on several occasions. And the text indicates that something about Jesus poked deep into Levi's heart. Levi sensed that God had something better for him. So, when Jesus comes along one day and says, "Levi, come with me," he says to the others collectors at the station, "Guys, cover me, will ya? I'm gonna be gone for a few hours." And just like that, he joins Jesus' band of followers.

The first few hours of following Jesus turns into a few days, and soon Levi's heart is changed. He is having conversations with some of his fellow tax collectors and with the few other people who would have anything to do with him. He is talking to prostitutes, adulterers, extortionists—people who were also looked upon as disreputable sinners—telling them what it had been like to spend the last few days with Jesus. When some of them asked if it would be okay for them to come along the next day to hear Jesus, Levi would have convinced them that Jesus wouldn't mind. And just like that, some of Levi's friends begin following Jesus.

After several days the text tells us that Levi decided to throw a party for Jesus at his house. He invited all his friends. That way Levi's friends could have Jesus to themselves. Now Jesus has not only invited this disreputable man to be his disciple, he actually commits to attending a party with a whole crowd of disreputable people! Why does Jesus make such a socially risky move? He has the eyes of a doctor. He sees their hurts that only God can heal. We read:

> While Jesus was having dinner at Levi's house, many tax collectors and sinners were eating with him and his disciples, for there were many who followed him. When the teachers of the law who were Pharisees saw him eating with the sinners and tax collectors, they asked his disciples: "Why does he eat with tax collectors and sinners?"
>
> On hearing this, Jesus said to them, "It is not the healthy who need a doctor, but the sick. I have not come to call the righteous, but sinners."[110]

The Pharisees objected to Jesus eating with such disreputable people. To them it implied acceptance of the sinners' lifestyle. Why was he partying with them? they wondered. And it was a party going on at Levi's house—no doubt about it! The words used in the text to describe the gathering are not the normal words for simply sitting at a table, having a nice meal. They are party words of that time—words that say they were all having a grand ole time! But as far as the Pharisees were concerned, Jesus was with the wrong people in the wrong place.

The Pharisees were a strict group in Israel who tried to follow the Old Testament laws to the nth degree—all in an effort to stay separated from any evil influence. Their motives were good, but the way they carried them out put unreasonable demands on those who would listen to them. They added things to the Old Testament law that were never there, and when people didn't measure up to their standards, they judged them, lumping them together—and dismissing them—as sinners.

You can imagine how horrifying it was for the Pharisees to see Jesus go into a house filled with sinners. Even worse, they could hear laughter coming from the house. So when the party finally broke up and Jesus and his disciples were coming out of the house, some of the Pharisees confronted Jesus' disciples, saying, "Why does he eat with tax collectors and sinners?"[111] Why is he associating with such disreputable people? They were not asking for information. They were saying this in an accusatory manner, insisting he should not be doing what he was doing.

The text tells us that Jesus overheard their question and gave them the answer that becomes our pattern of behavior for today: "It is not the healthy who need a doctor, but the sick. I have not come to call the righteous, but sinners."[112] Jesus is saying that it makes as much sense for us to stay away from sinners as it does for a doctor to stay away from the sick. A doctor must go out among the sick in order to bring healing, just as we go out among the sinners to proclaim an even deeper healing that comes from God.

CONCLUSION

So, yes! By all means! Move into their world with the eyes of a doctor, seeing the hurts that God can heal. Talk to the Goth girl. Strike up a small friendship. As Christmas draws closer, buy her a present—one of the new thermoses Starbucks is selling. Have lunch with the dead-beat dad. If there's an unmarried pregnant girl in one of your crowded classes, save a seat. Strike up a conversation with the older woman on the prowl for another man. Engage with the man who has just lost his license for drunk driving. If your coworkers invite you, join the softball team. Go with them to the karaoke clubs and attend the company New Year's Eve party. Stay sober, but sit and talk and laugh. Go to the high school reunions. Tell stories about whose houses you used to TP or about how your team won the district championship that year. Marvel that Mr. Brewer is still teaching algebra. Take some chips and dip to the tailgate parties. When they start talking about women, brag about your wife and tell them she's the best thing that ever happened to you. Tell them at the end of the night that you'd love to go again with them next week—except that you and your wife are going on a couples' retreat with your church.

Move into their world and connect if they're willing. Be a friend, and let God take it from there. Move into their world with the eyes of a doctor, seeing the hurts that God can heal.

NOTES

Introduction
1. John 14:5 NIV.
2. Proverbs 16:9 NASB.

Part I: Road Worthy
3. Jeremiah 12:5 NLT.

The Need for Honest Self-Assessment
4. William Wilberforce quotes and stories in this chapter are from Garth Lean, *God's Politician: William Wilberforce's Struggle* (Colorado Springs: Helmers & Howard, 1987).
5. Anthony Bloom, *Beginning to Pray* (New York: Paulist Press, 1970), 86.
6. Psalm 43:5 NKJV.
7. Psalm 139:3 NKJV.
8. Genesis 4:6 NIV.
9. 1 Kings 19:13 NIV.
10. 2 Corinthians 12:8 NIV.
11. Henri J. Nouwen, *The Living Reminder: Service and Prayer in Memory of Jesus Christ* (New York: HarperCollins, 1977), 11.
12. "Where the Battle's Lost and Won," December 27, 2012, selection, *My Utmost for His Highest Classic Edition*, Daily Devotionals by Oswald Chambers website, http://utmost.org/classic/where-the-battle%E2%80%99s-lost-and-won-classic/
13. Exodus 33:11 NLT.
14. 2 Corinthians 13:5 MSG.
15. Jonathan Aitkin, *John Newton: From Disgrace to Amazing Grace* (Wheaton, IL: Crossway, 2007), 116.

Look at Yourself First
16. 1 Samuel 30:6 NASB.
17. Acts 20:24.

Avoiding Cultural Contamination
18. Jonah 1:9 NIV.
19. Zechariah 8:23 NASB.

The Fall
20. View the video of Conrad's fall at: http://vimeo.com/20549603
21. Pete Scazzero, *The Emotionally Healthy Church: A Strategy for Discipleship That Actually Changes Lives* (Grand Rapids, MI: Zondervan, 2010), 148.

Part II: Necessary Repairs
22. Revelation 3:17 NIV.

Sharpen Your Sixth Sense
23. Luke 10:7 KJV.
24. Romans 8:14 NIV.

Reading the Bible Spiritually

25. Richard J. Foster, *Life with God: Reading the Bible for Spiritual Transformation* (San Francisco: HarperOne, 2008), 62–63.

Tame the Restless Evil

26. Proverbs 17:27 NIV1984.

27. Proverbs 17:28 NIV1984.

28. Proverbs 16:28 NIV1984.

29. Proverbs 17:9 NIV1984.

30. Proverbs 18:13 NIV1984.

31. Proverbs 14:3 NIV1984.

32. Proverbs 17:27 NIV1984.

33. Proverbs 15:23 NIV1984.

34. Proverbs 15:1 NIV1984.

35. Proverbs 18:21 NIV1984.

36. Proverbs 13:3 NIV1984.

37. Proverbs 10:19 NIV1984.

Part III: Washouts and Detours

38. "Washington Bridge Collapse Caused by Truck Hitting Span, Authorities Say," FoxNews.com, May 24, 2013, http://www.foxnews.com/us/2013/05/24/highway-bridge-collapses-in-washington-state-people-in-water/

39. John 16:33 NIV.

Trouble Happens

40. Job 1:21 ESV.

41. Job 42:5 NIV.

42. Job 1:20 ESV.

43. David Jackson, *Crying Out for Vindication: The Gospel According to Job, Gospel According to the Old Testament* (Phillipsburg, NJ: P & R, 2007), 1.

44. Job 1:22 ESV.

45. Job 1:20 ESV.

46. Romans 8:23 NKJV.

47. Job 1:20 NKJV.

48. Job 1:21 NKJV.

49. 2 Corinthians 4:8 RSV.

50. 2 Corinthians 4:16 RSV.

51. 2 Corinthians 4:18 RSV.

52. Philippians 1:21 RSV.

The Art of Managing Conflict

53. Acts 6:1–6.

54. 1 Peter 5:8.

Bad Situations Are Great Opportunities

55. Philippians 2:5–8.

56. Acts 16:30 NIV.

MLOLTER

TTRA

57. Acts 16:31 NIV.

58. Luke 24:41 NIV.

59. Acts 16:25 NIV.

60. Acts 16:28–30 NIV.

61. Acts 16:17 NIV.

62. Quoted in Os Guinness, *The Call: Finding and Fulfilling the Central Purpose for Your Life* (Nashville: Thomas Nelson, 2003), 101.

Part IV: Traveling Light

63. Galatians 5:16; 1 Peter 5:7 NKJV.

A Steady Rhythm

64. Mark 6:31 NET.

65. Proverbs 10:19 NET.

66. Psalm 4:4–5 NRSV.

The Crucial Need for Regular Rest

67. Herman Wouk, *This Is My God* (New York: Doubleday, 1959; repr. New York: Back Bay Books, 1992), 44–45. Citations refer to the Back Bay edition.

68. Ibid., 45.

69. Ibid., 46.

70. Ibid.

71. Ibid.

72. Ibid.

73. Ibid.

74. Jonathan Sacks, *Faith in the Future: Rediscovering the Beauty of the Sabbath* (Macon, GA: Mercer University Press, 1995), 133.

75. Ibid.

76. Joseph Lieberman, *The Gift of Rest* (Brentwood, TN: Howard Books, 2011), 3.

77. Ibid.

78. Cf. Isaiah 6:5.

79. Psalm 100:2–3 NIV.

Striving for Simplicity

80. Matthew 6:24–25, 32 NLT.

81. 1 Timothy 6:9–10 NLT.

82. Nehemiah 2:12.

83. Genesis 3:1 NLT.

84. Genesis 2:16–17 NLT.

85. Isaiah 22:13; 1 Corinthians 15:32 TLB.

86. Hebrews 13:5 TLB.

Mentoring Others to Spiritual Maturity

87. Richard J. Foster, *Celebration of Discipline: The Path to Spiritual Growth,* 3rd ed. (San Francisco: HarperSanFrancisco, 2002), 1.

88. Colossians 2:7 NIV.

89. Acts 22:3 NIV1984.

90. Luke 5:8 NKJV.

91. Luke 5:10 NKJV.

92. Philippians 3:10 NIV.

93. Luke 8:25; Matthew 14:16; Matthew 26:31; Matthew 16:23; Luke 24:17; Luke 9:60.

94. John 15:15; John 16:7; John 14:12; John 13:34; Mark 16:15.

95. Cf. 2 Timothy 2:2.

96. 1 Timothy 4:12 NIV.

97. John 17:6, 8, 15, 17, 18.

Yield the Right of Way

98. Eugene H. Peterson, *The Pastor: A Memoir*, repr. ed. (New York: HarperOne, 2012), 46–48.

99. Matthew 5:17.

100. "Why Jesus Called a Man a Fool," in *A Knock at Midnight: Inspiration from the Great Sermons of Reverend Martin Luther King, Jr.*, eds. Clayborne Carson and Peter Holloran (New York: Warner Books, 2000), 162.

101. Romans 8:31 NIV.

102. Martin Luther King, Jr., *Stride toward Freedom: The Montgomery Story*, ed. Clayborne Carson (1958; repr., Boston: Beacon Press, 2010), 128.

103. Ibid., 129.

The First Rule of the Road: Love

104. John 13:35 NIV1984.

105. Matthew 23:23 NIV.

106. C. S. Lewis, *The Four Loves* (New York: Harcourt, Brace & World, 1960), 168.

107. Romans 8:1 RSV.

108. 1 John 4:19.

109. John 3:16.

See with the Eyes of a Doctor

110. Mark 2:15–17 NIV.

111. Mark 2:16 NIV.

112. Mark 2:17 NIV.

WORTHY
PUBLISHING

IF YOU ENJOYED THIS BOOK, WILL YOU CONSIDER
SHARING THE MESSAGE WITH OTHERS?

- Mention the book in a Facebook post, Twitter update, Pinterest pin, or blog post.

- Recommend this book to those in your small group, book club, workplace, and classes.

- Head over to facebook.com/worthypublishing, "LIKE" the page, and post a comment as to what you enjoyed the most.

- Tweet "I recommend reading #roadwemusttravel from @worthypub"

- Pick up a copy for someone you know who would be challenged and encouraged by this message.

- Write a book review online.

You can subscribe to Worthy Publishing's newsletter at worthypublishing.com.

WORTHY PUBLISHING
FACEBOOK PAGE

WORTHY PUBLISHING
WEBSITE